Top 25 locator map
(continues on inside
back cover)
◄

KT-367-189

CityPack
Florence

SUSANNAH PERRY

AA Publishing
Find out more about AA Publishing and the
wide range of services the AA provides by
visiting our website at *www.theAA.com*

About this Book

✚	Map reference to the accompanying fold-out map, and Top 25 locator map	⛴	Nearest riverboat or ferry stop
✉	Address	♿	Facilities for visitors with disabilities
☎	Telephone number	✋	Admission charge
🕐	Opening/closing times	↔	Other nearby places of interest
🍴	Restaurant or café on premises or nearby	❓	Tours, lectures or special events
🚆	Nearest railway station	➤	Indicates the page where you will find a fuller description
🚌	Nearest bus route	ℹ	Tourist information

ORGANISATION

CityPack Florence is divided into six sections:

- Planning Ahead and Getting There
- Living Florence – Florence Now, Florence Then, Time to Shop, Out and About, Walks, Florence by Night
- Florence's Top 25 Sights
- Florence's Best – best of the rest
- Where to – detailed listings of restaurants, hotels, shops and nightlife
- Travel facts – packed with practical information

In addition, easy-to-read side panels provide extra facts and snippets, highlights of places to visit and invaluable practical advice.

MAPS

The fold-out map in the wallet at the back of the book is a comprehensive street plan of Florence. The first (or only) map reference given for each attraction refers to this map. **The Top 25 locator maps** found on the inside front and back covers of the book itself are for quick reference. They show the Top 25 Sights, described on pages 26–50, which are clearly plotted by number (**1**–**25**, not page number) across the city. The second map reference given for the Top 25 Sights refers to this map.

ADMISSION CHARGES

An indication of the admission charge for sights is given by categorising the standard adult rate as follows:
✋ Expensive (over 5 euros/L10,000), Moderate (3–5 euros/L6–10,000) and Inexpensive (3 euros/L6,000 or less).

Contents

Planning Ahead...

WHEN TO GO

Florence's peak season runs from February to October, although many consider it virtually uninterrupted. The city is overrun with tour groups in June and July. If you like heat, go in August – although many Florentines are on holiday and some restaurants close, it's a good time to go because everything is quieter.

TIME

Italy is one hour ahead of Greenwich Mean Time (two hours ahead from late March to October).

AVERAGE DAILY TEMPERATURES

JAN	FEB	MAR	APR	MAY	JUN	JUL	AUG	SEP	OCT	NOV	DEC
10°C	11°C	15°C	18°C	23°C	26°C	29°C	28°C	26°C	21°C	14°C	12°C

Spring (March to May) is a good time to visit if you want to avoid the summer heat.
Summer (June to August) can be extremely hot and humid, sometimes uncomfortably so during July and August.
Autumn (September to November) is generally the wettest time in Tuscany, and thunderstorms are common in September.
Winter (December to February) temperatures are often similar to those in northern European countries, and rainfall can be high.

WHAT'S ON

January *Pitti Immagine*: Fashion shows at the Fortezza da Basso.

February *Carnevale*: A low-key version of Venice's annual extravaganza.

March *Festa dell'Annunziata* (25 Mar): Traditionally the Florentine new year, with a fair to celebrate in Piazza Santissima Annunziata.
Scoppio del Carro: The Easter Sunday service at the Duomo culminates in an exploding carriage full of fireworks.

April *Mostra Mercato Internazionale dell' Artigianato*: An international arts and crafts festival in the Fortezza da Basso.

May *Maggio Musicale*: Florence's international music and dance festival.
Festa del Grillo (Sun after Ascension): Crickets are sold in cages, then released in the park of Le Cascine (➤ 58).

June *Calcio in Costume*: An elaborate football game between town districts played in medieval costume in Piazza Santa Croce (➤ 49, 85); preceded by a procession.
Festa di San Giovanni (24 Jun): Fireworks are set off in Piazzale Michelangelo to celebrate the feast of the patron saint of Florence.
Estate Fiesolana (mid-Jun to Aug): A Fiesole arts festival (➤ 82).

September *Festa del Rificolona* (7 Sep): Children carry paper lanterns in Piazza Santissima Annunziata to honour the birth of the Virgin.

October *Amici della Musica* (Oct–Apr): Concerts. Tickets from Teatro della Pergola (☎ 055 608 420).

November *Festival dei Popoli* (Nov–Dec): A film festival in the Palazzo dei Congressi, showing international films.

4

FLORENCE ONLINE

www.enit.it
Florence is particularly well covered on the Italian Tourist Board website, with information on history, culture, events, accommodation and gastronomy, in several languages.

www.turismo.toscana.it
This site is run by the Tuscan Regional Tourist Board and covers the whole region as well as Florence, the capital. Beautifully designed, with an English-language option, it has information ranging from the practical to the esoteric, and an easy-to-use search facility.

www.comune.firenze.it
Florence City Council aims its website primarily at locals, but its tourism, museum and art pages are always up to date and it has some good links. Italian only.

www.firenze.net
This Florence-based site, in Italian and English, has information on where to go and what to do, with good maps and plenty of links.

www.emmeti.it
Another Italy-based site, in Italian and English, with a good range of information and links for Florence. It is strong on local events and has an online hotel reservation service.

www.initaly.com
This lively US site is clearly run by passionate Italophiles and has excellent planning tips and sightseeing hints.

www.promhotels.it
Useful online hotel booking site for Florence and other Italian destinations.

www.florenceart.it
You can pre-book a timed entrance ticket and jump the queues to the main Florentine museums (Uffizi, Accademia, Medici Chapels, San Marco, Bargello) via this efficient site.

GOOD TRAVEL SITES

www.fodors.com
A complete travel-planning site. You can research prices and weather; book air tickets, cars and rooms; ask questions (and get answers) from fellow travellers; and find links to other sites.

www.fs-on-line.it
The official site of the Italian State Railways.

www.weatheronline.co.uk /Italy
Good three-day weather predictions.

CYBERCAFÉS

Internet Train
✚ bIII ✉ Via dell' Orinolo 25r ☎ 055 263 8968 ◷ Mon–Fri 10–10:30, Sat 10–8, Sun 3–7 💷 6 euros/L12,000 per hour.

The NetGate
✚ bII ✉ Via Cavour 14r ☎ 055 210 004 ◷ Daily 10–8 💷 5 euros/L10,000 per hour.

Popcafé
✚ aIV ✉ Piazza Santo Spirito 18a/r ☎ 055 211 201 ◷ Noon–2AM 💷 5 euros/L10,000 per hour.

…and Getting There

FLIGHTS FROM OUTSIDE EUROPE

There are no direct intercontinental flights to Florence so visitors from outside Europe fly to Milan (298km north), Rome (277km south) or another European city, then take a connecting flight or train. The flight from New York to Rome takes around nine hours. From the airport, take a shuttle train to Stazione Termini, then a train to Florence (two hours).

MONEY

The euro is the official currency of Italy. Bank notes in denominations of 5, 10, 20, 50, 100, 200 and 500 euros and coins in denominations of 1, 2, 5, 10, 20 and 50 cents, and 1 and 2 euros, were introduced on 1 January 2002.

50 euros

200 euros

500 euros

ARRIVING

You can choose from three airports – Galileo Galilei Airport at Pisa, the small Amerigo Vespucci Airport at Florence and Guglielmo Marconi Airport at Bologna. The flight takes approximately 2 hours from London.

120KM

Bologna Airport
105km to Florence
Bus then train, 1 hour+
12.50 euros

Florence Airport
6km to city centre
Bus, 20 minutes
3 euros

Pisa Airport
80km to Florence
Train, 1 hour
4.70 euros

FROM FLORENCE AIRPORT

Amerigo Vespucci Airport (☎ 055 373 498; www.safnet.it), also known as La Peretola, is connected to the city centre by blue SITA buses, which run every 30 minutes between 6AM and 8:30PM, then every hour until 11PM. The journey takes 20 minutes and tickets, which cost 3 euros/L6,000, can be bought on board. Taxis cost around 15 euros/L30,000, plus possible surcharges (confirm the fare with the driver before you set off). Hire cars are available.

FROM PISA AIRPORT

From Pisa's Galileo Galilei Airport (☎ 050 500 707; www.pisa-airport.com) 11 trains a day leave for Florence between 8:49AM and around 7PM. The journey takes an hour and costs around 4.70 euros/L9,100. Additional trains leave from Pisa Centrale station, a 10-minute taxi ride away. Car hire is available. A taxi to Florence costs around 129 euros/L250,000.

FROM BOLOGNA AIRPORT

From Guglielmo Marconi Airport (☎ 051 647 9615; www.bologna-airport.it) a shuttle bus takes passengers to Bologna Centrale station, costing 2.50 euros/L5,000. From here trains to Florence run roughly every half hour; the journey takes just over an hour and costs around 10 euros/L20,000. Hire cars are available in Terminal A. A taxi to Florence costs around 196 euros/L380,000.

Arriving by Train
The main station, Santa Maria Novella, has train links with major Italian cities as well as Paris, Ostend and Frankfurt. Most buses in Florence depart from the station forecourt, and there are usually taxis waiting. Don't forget to validate your ticket before boarding your train. Do this by inserting the ticket into the orange box on the platform.

Arriving by Long-Distance Bus
Lazzi runs express services to and from Rome and links Florence with major European cities (⊠ Piazza della Stazione 47 ☎ 055 351 061).

Getting Around
Bus routes in Florence are numbered and many start and end at the railway station at regular intervals. Zippy little electric buses, identified by letters (A–D), link all kinds of places in the narrow streets of the old centre which were previously inaccessible by public transport. Buy tickets at bars and tobacconists before boarding. Once on board, insert your ticket into the small orange box and it will be stamped with the time. The ticket is valid for the next 60 minutes for any bus. Failure to validate your ticket can result in a hefty fine. The tourist information office by the station has bus maps.

Taxis
Official Florentine taxis are comfortable, clean and white. You can hail them from central places such as the station or Piazza del Duomo, or call one of the official cab companies: Radio Taxi SO.CO.TA. (☎ 055 4798/4242) or Radio Taxi CO.TA.FI. (☎ 055 4390). The meter starts running the moment the call is received. Supplements are charged for baggage and for journeys at night.

ENTRY REQUIREMENTS

Anyone entering Italy must have a valid passport (or official identity card for EU nationals).

INSURANCE

Travel insurance with an option that covers theft of cash is indispensable; pickpockets are rife.

VISITORS WITH DISABILITIES

As in many other historic Italian cities, travellers with disabilities are far from well served in Florence, though things are slowly improving. The tourist office provides a booklet detailing facilities for people with disabilities in local buildings. Many city museums are fully wheelchair-accessible, with ramps, lifts and appropriate lavatories. The grey and green buses can take wheelchairs, as does the electric D bus, which goes through the centre of Florence (board via the electric platform at the rear door). Taxis take wheelchairs but it is wise to let them know when you book.

Living
Florence

Florence Now

Piazza della Signoria hosts the opening ceremony of the Calcio in Costume
Above right: shoppers and sightseers on the Ponte Vecchio

Florence, the Cradle of the Renaissance, pulls in millions of visitors each year, drawn by a dream of artistic perfection and hoping for a blast of aesthetic magic. This little city contributed more to European culture than anywhere else during the 14th and 15th centuries, exploding in a creative frenzy that can be experienced to this day in the architecture, paintings and sculptures.

You'll find Florence rich in reminders of its golden age – the city centre has changed little since the great construction works of the Renaissance. Harmonious *palazzi* line the narrow streets and monumental civic buildings and splendid churches dominate the public squares. The surrounding hills form the perfect

NEIGHBOURHOODS

• The heart of Florence is the square grid of streets laid out by the Romans: here the religious centre, Piazza del Duomo, is closely linked to the political centre, Piazza della Signoria. In the east, Santa Croce is historically the working-class area, while the ultra-glamorous Via de' Tornabuoni is in the west. Across the river, the Oltrarno (literally 'beyond the Arno') is the site of the Pitti Palace and the Boboli Gardens. It is also the most relaxed part of city, least touched by tourism.

backdrop to the restrained elegance of the cityscape. Nonetheless, learning to love the world's greatest collection of Renaissance art can be hard work – Florence is small, crowded and noisy, jammed with traffic and so swamped with tourists that it is easy to dismiss it as a sort of cultural theme park.

It's not. Briefly the capital of Italy, Florence is still the capital of Tuscany, one of Italy's richest regions. The city is home to a major university, as well as numerous other academic institutions, many associated with the fine arts. There are workshops and laboratories dedicated to art restoration and a higher proportion of skilled artisans than in almost any other Italian city. Florence has a long tradition of involvement in fashion, a spin-off from its centuries-old leather industry. The sprawling western outskirts are scattered with light industry. This is a prosperous, thriving city, and although tourism is the major industry, it is far from the only one.

Below: sculpture by Giambologna in Piazza della Signoria

Above: *an arcade behind the Mercato Centrale*

For visitors, prices are high, but not too high. Hotels and restaurants provide what their customers want. Museums have been revamped wherever possible. Shopping is taken seriously – after all, this is Italy. Getting around is easy; the city centre is tiny and you can walk nearly everywhere. This has become much more pleasant in recent years, with the pedestrianisation of the area from the Duomo south through the Piazza della Signoria to the Ponte Vecchio and east from the Signoria to Santa Croce.

However, the sheer number of tourists can make walking painfully slow, and in parts of the *centro storico* it's rare to hear Italian spoken. The authorities are aware of this, but are caught in a cleft stick – Florence depends on tourism. Plans for a visitor tax have been mooted, but little progress made towards a solution.

Yet the Florentines have no intention of killing the goose that lays the golden egg, and have poured money into doing whatever's possible to make to the city visitor-friendly. The city's great 20th-century planning triumph was the preservation of the outlying hills, leaving a green ring

LEFT-LEANING

• Tuscany is probably the only place in Europe where you will still find communist posters and graffiti on the street corners. Florence, the capital of Tuscany, is no exception, and many Florentines cling tenaciously to the icons of their left-wing identity.

Above: *early evening on Ponte Santa Trinita*
Left: *detail, Neptune's Fountain, Piazza della Signoria*

encircling three sides of Florence. Few other European cities have preserved their immediate surroundings better. This means that in even the busiest months of the year it is possible to escape the crowds. Close to the city lies some of Italy's most beautiful countryside, a dreamy

THE MEDICI

• The Medici family were virtual sovereigns of Florence from the 14th to the 18th century, playing a pivotal role in the city's history. Cosimo il Vecchio emerged in the 1430s as the first major player, becoming the pre-eminent political figure in Florence. Influence was maintained under his son, Piero, and grandson, Lorenzo il Magnifico, a great humanist and artistic patron. The family were temporarily out of power from 1494 to 1512, but became Grand Dukes of Tuscany in 1570. As trade shifted north in the 18th century, Tuscany's power and profits dwindled. One of the last of the Medici family, the drunken Gian Gastone, died in 1737, leaving Tuscany to the House of Lorraine and his family's incomparable art collections to his sister, Anna Maria. This enlightened lady bequeathed them in perpetuity to the city of Florence.

THE UFFIZI BOMBING

• In 1993 a huge bomb exploded on the west side of the Uffizi, killing five people, causing structural harm to the building, destroying the Gregoriophilus Library and damaging numerous pictures. Once thought to have been the work of the Mafia, the crime remains unsolved and the culprits have never been caught.

13

Above: *relaxing in one of Piazza della Signoria's cafés*
Right: *inside the Duomo*
Far right: *scooters are popular in Florence, where the roads are narrow and parking is restricted*

landscape of rolling hills dotted with villages and punctuated by solitary cypresses. Many visitors choose to stay outside Florence, using efficient public transport to come in for sightseeing. Those based in the city can take excursions to quieter Tuscan towns, just as the Florentines themselves do. During the winter months fewer people throng the streets, museums are less crowded and churches are relatively quiet.

The vital point to bear in mind is that Florence should be a pleasure, not a cultural marathon. So concentrate on what appeals to you – see what you want to see not what you think

ON THE BALL

• The Medici family left their mark on every building owned by or connected with them, so look out for their coat of arms, a varying number of balls (*palle*) on a shield, on buildings everywhere. The *palle* probably represent either pills or coins, references to their original trade as apothecaries and later role as bankers.

you should see, even if it's just one church and one museum. There's more pleasure to be had in exploring the quiet streets of the Oltrarno, crammed with little workshops and local shops, than queuing for three hours to jostle for two minutes in front of a Botticelli masterpiece. A leisurely picnic, its ingredients fresh from the market, in the green oasis of the Boboli Gardens will be infinitely more memorable than an over-priced pizza in a hot and crowded bar. If you do want to saturate yourself with Renaissance art, do your planning. Book ahead to avoid queues and start early, taking long lunchtime closing into account.

Florence retains its Tuscan character, even though every year sees a rise in visitor numbers. The citizens are well aware of their patrimony and have no doubt they live in one of the world's great cities. It's up to you to get beneath the bewilderingly crowded surface of Florence to the beautiful heart beneath.

VITAL STATISTICS

● While Florence attracts around 7 million visitors a year, the native population currently hovers around 400,000.

● Florence has one of the lowest birth rates in Italy, which has the lowest national birth rate in the world.

● The Uffizi Gallery is Italy's most visited museum.

● Florence is on the same latitude as Toronto, in Canada, and Sapporo, in Japan.

15

Florence Then

BEFORE 1000

Florence started to grow in 59 BC as a result of an agrarian law passed by Julius Caesar, granting land to retired army veterans. Byzantine walls were added to the Roman walls in AD 541–44, as protection against the Ostrogoths.
The Lombards took Tuscany in 570 but were defeated in the early 9th century by Charlemagne. Florence became part of the Holy Roman Empire, ruled by imperial princes known as Margraves.

THE FLORIN

Florence minted its own coins, florins, in silver in 1235 and in gold in 1252. Soon they were being used as the standard coin in Europe, evidence of the pre-eminence of Florence in European finance.

1115 The first *comune* (city state) is formed. Florence is run by a 100-strong assembly.

1250–60 The *Primo Popolo* regime controls Florence, dominated by trade guilds.

1296 The building of the Duomo begins, under Arnolfo di Cambio.

1340s Florence faces economic crisis after Edward III of England bankrupts the Peruzzi and Bardi and the Black Death plague halves the population.

1378 The uprising of the *ciompi* (wool carders) is the high point of labour unrest.

1406 Florence captures Pisa, gaining direct access to the sea.

1458 Cosimo de' Medici is recognised as ruler of Florence.

1469–92 Lorenzo the Magnificent rules.

1478 Pazzi conspirators seem to have Giuliano and Lorenzo murdered in the cathedral. Giuliano is killed but Lorenzo escapes.

1494 Florence surrenders to Charles VIII of France. Savonarola, a zealous monk, takes control of the city.

1498 Savonarola is burned at the stake after four years of rule, and Florence becomes a republic.

1502 The Republic of Florence retakes Pisa.

1570 Cosimo I creates a Tuscan state free from the Holy Roman Empire.

1743 Anna Maria Luisa, last of the Medici, dies. Florence is then ruled by the house of Lorraine under Francis Stephen.

1799– Tuscany is occupied by Napoleon's
1814 troops.

1865–70 Florence becomes capital of Italy. King Vittorio Emanuele is installed in Pitti Palace.

1944 On 4 August, Germans blow up all the bridges in Florence except the Ponte Vecchio.

1966 The River Arno bursts its banks: Florence is flooded.

1993 The Uffizi Gallery is bombed.

1996 The G7 meeting is held in Florence.

2002 Euro notes and coins are introduced across Italy.

Above (left to right): *Niccolò Machiavelli; a 1554 plan of Florence; the destruction of Ponte Santa Trinita in 1944; the floods of 1966*

FLORENCE PEOPLE

The poet Dante Alighieri, author of the *Divine Comedy*, was born in Florence in 1265. He was exiled from the city in 1302 because of his sympathies with the White Guelphs, and died in 1321.

Michelangelo Buonarroti (1475–1564) created some of his most famous works in Florence, including the sculpture *David*. Born in Caprese, he was buried in Florence's Santa Croce.

Political philosopher Niccolò Machiavelli was born in Florence in 1469.

Galileo Galilei (1564–1642), from Pisa, spent much of his life in Florence as the Medici court mathematician.

17

Time to Shop

Florence is high on every foreign shopper's itinerary, but it's also a big attraction for Italians, who rate it highly for leather goods, fabrics, bed linens, lingerie, china and ceramics. As Tuscany's capital, Florence has the pick of Tuscan goods and shops, and people come from all over the

STREET TRADE

Street trading is an essential part of the Florentine scene, with tourists being offered everything from fake designer bags to lighters and African artefacts. Some traders are unlicensed and keep a constant eye open for approaching *carabinieri*, ready to scoop up their merchandise and run. Unless you want to buy, don't stop and look; if you do, you'll be a prime target, engaged on a protracted haggle which should get the price down by about two thirds. A number of traders are from North Africa and Senegal, often students or graduates who aim to make enough money in a few years in Italy to secure their financial future at home.

region for a wider choice than they'll find at home. In the era of the global market, much of what's on sale is available worldwide, but the choice is wider and the prices often lower for many Italian essentials.

The nicest souvenirs are often everyday items – kitchenware, household linens, tools and quirky stationery. Head for the markets for good value espresso coffee makers and the tiny cups to go with them, wonderful gadgets such as fish-scalers and primitive grids for making toast over an open flame, and vividly coloured plastic goods. Plastic also features heavily in the cheap and cheerful children's toys; best values are often in tiny shops away from the main streets. Food is a favourite take-home; you could consider more prosaic goods than expensive oils and wine – how about herb packs specially blended for different foods, the excellent stock cubes known as *dadi* or sachets of vanilla sugar?

One of Florence's major attractions is the wealth of artisan workshops, clustered mainly across the river in the Oltrarno area. Many specialise in antique restoration for the city's numerous dealers, but there's more. Look for picture framers where you can get new purchases

Fresh produce and leather goods are in plentiful supply in Florence's markets, but you may also find more unusual souvenirs, like this 'Duomo' umbrella (below)

mounted, shoemakers selling wonderful velvet pads and brushes for achieving that special shine and marble-paper makers where you may have a chance to watch the whole creative process.

Prints, books and old maps and city plans make special souvenirs, and there's also a wide range of cookbooks on Tuscan cuisine, many in English. Beautiful calendars with views of Florence and Tuscany are on sale as early as April for the following year. The museum shops are good for these too.

There's no chance that you'll be overwhelmed by good taste either; there are T-shirts bearing images of Michelangelo and Botticelli, plastic models of the Duomo and Ponte Vecchio, grotesque ceramics and fakes of every description. Where else could you buy a silvery reproduction of Michelangelo's *David*, complete with twinkling lights?

CHIC ON THE CHEAP

Markets are the best source of cheap and second-hand clothing with an Italian twist. The weekly Cascine market (➤ 62, 75) is where the Florentines go for bargains – dive into the most crowded stalls. Gucci's shop in Via Aretina stocks unsold sale items at reductions of about a third and the area around San Lorenzo is good trawling ground for up-to-the-minute, cheap and cheerful designs.

Out and About

20

INFORMATION

FIESOLE
Distance 8km
Journey Time 20–30 minutes
🚌 7 (buses depart from Santa Maria Novella station or San Marco)
ℹ️ Piazza Mino 37
☎ 055 598 720

SIENA
Distance 66km
Journey Time 1–2 hours
🚆 Regular departures from Santa Maria Novella station
ℹ️ Piazza del Campo 56
☎ 0577 280 551

Left to right: an exhibit from the Roman and Etruscan Museum, Fiesole; the Piazza del Campo, Siena; the Leaning Tower of Pisa

GUIDED TOURS

Bus tours are available from Florence to Pisa, Chianti, San Gimignano and Siena, run by:

CAF
✉️ Via Roma 4
☎ 055 210 612
SITA
✉️ Via Santa Caterina da Siena 15r
☎ 055 483 651
Lazzi
✉️ Piazza della Stazione
☎ 055 351 061

EXCURSIONS
FIESOLE

Fiesole is a charming hill town just above Florence, and more important than Florence for much of the Roman period. It has a Roman theatre and impressive Etruscan remains. It is

easily accessible and a delightfully quiet place to escape to from Florence. The bus from Florence arrives in Fiesole's Piazza Mino. (The last bus returns to Florence at 1AM, allowing an evening visit to admire the lights in the city below.) The Roman ruins are clearly signposted, and the ticket includes access to the Roman and Etruscan museum. There is a small Romanesque cathedral dating from the 11th century. Walk up the Via di San Francesco for wonderful views of Florence. Walk or take bus No. 7 down the hill to the village of San Domenico, and from there walk to the Badia Fiesolana, a pretty Romanesque church with an inlaid façade.

SIENA

One of the loveliest towns in Italy, with great museums, fabulous shops and many hills, Siena is best reached by train. At Siena station take the shuttle bus to the centre and spend the rest of the day on foot. The focal point is the fan-shaped Piazza del Campo, which slopes down to the bell tower. The Gothic cathedral was built between 1136 and 1382. Outside is a vast unfinished nave, begun in 1339 with the intention of making this the world's largest cathedral. Work was abandoned during the plague of 1348. Look for the animal symbols of the town's 17 *contrade* (districts) that take part in the famous *Palio*, a fearsome horse race held in the Piazza del Campo on 2 July and 16 August (► 85).

THE TUSCAN COUNTRYSIDE

A country drive is a real treat. Much-visited San Gimignano is a prime destination with its hilltop site and medieval towers. Its Palazzo del Popolo houses a gruesome museum of torture. For lovely pots, stop in Montelupo, where many of Florence's ceramics have been made for centuries. On your way back visit Vinci, to the west of Florence, the birthplace of Leonardo da Vinci (1452–1519); it is home to a museum about his life, art and inventions. Enjoy the views and perhaps buy some olive oil and wine from a farm. If you want a swim, the village of Sambuca, near Tavarnelle, has an excellent outdoor pool.

PISA

Pisa's main draw is the stunning architectural ensemble known as the Campo dei Miracoli (Field of Miracles), home to the famous Leaning Tower. This beautiful structure, which re-opened in 2001 after years of work to steady the tilt, stands next to the Romanesque-Gothic Duomo and Baptistery, the largest in Italy. All three buildings date from the 11th and 12th centuries, the time of Pisa's economic and political heyday.

INFORMATION

Car hire (► 91)

SAN GIMIGNANO
Distance 57km
Journey Time 1 hour
Route Take the Firenze/Siena *raccordo* (a motorway link road) until the Poggibonsi exit. Follow the signs from here to San Gimignano (around 6km)

Museo Leonardiano
✉ Castello dei Conti Guidi, Vinci
☎ 0571 56055
⊙ Mar–Oct: daily 9:30–7. Nov–Feb: daily 9:30–6
🎟 Moderate

INFORMATION

PISA
Distance 80km
Journey Time 1 hour
🚆 Regular departures from Santa Maria Novella station to Pisa Centrale Station
ℹ Piazza del Duomo
☎ 050 560 464

21

Walks

INFORMATION

Distance 2km
Time at least 2-3 hours
Start point
★ Ponte Vecchio
🚏 bIV
🚌 B, C
End point Piazzale Michelangelo
🚏 J7
🚌 12, 13

Piazza di Santa Felicità
Ponte Vecchio
Arno

Oltrarno

Piazzale Michelangelo

Porta di San Giorgio

Forte di Belvedere

Santa Felicità

San Miniato al Monte

0   200 m
0   200 yards

PONTE VECCHIO TO PIAZZALE MICHELANGELO

In summer this walk can be baking hot and it is best to start either very early in the morning or in the afternoon, about 4PM. Take a bottle of water along with you. In the spring or autumn plan a midday picnic at the Forte di Belvedere.

Start at the Ponte Vecchio and cross over to the Oltrarno. The first square on your left is Piazza di Santa Felicità, where you will find Pontormo's *Deposition* in Santa Felicità church (➤ 55). Take the road on the left of the church, the Costa di San Giorgio, where Galileo lived at No. 19. Continue up its steep slope, passing through Porta di San Giorgio (1260), the oldest city gate, with a carving of St George slaying the dragon.

Turn right into the Forte di Belvedere (➤ 57), which dates from 1590. Follow Via del Belvedere, which descends sharply along the city walls. At the bottom of the hill turn right into Via del Monte alle Croci. Follow it to its end then cross Viale Galileo Galilei to take the steps flanked by cypress trees and reliefs of the stations of the cross that continue up towards San Miniato (➤ 50). After your visit, go back to Viale Galileo Galilei, turn right and follow it to Piazzale Michelangelo for great views. A 12 or 13 bus will take you back to the centre of town.

DANTE'S FLORENCE

Start at the Baptistery, where the poet Dante Alighieri was baptised. Then, it was not covered with the marble facing. According to tradition, Dante watched the construction of the cathedral from the Sasso di Dante, a stone (marked) in the wall between Via dello Studio and Via del Proconsolo, opposite the Duomo.

Take the Via dello Studio. Turn left when you reach the Via del Corso and take the first right into Via di Santa Margherita. This leads to the Casa di Dante, which houses exhibits relating to 13th-century Florence. Immediately opposite is the church of San Martino del Vescovo, where Dante's family worshipped, and back towards Via del Corso is the church of Santa Margherita, where his lifelong muse, Beatrice, went to Mass.

From Santa Margherita turn left into Via Dante Alighieri for the entrance of the Badia, where Dante often saw Beatrice. The Badia's bell would have punctuated Dante's daily life. Exit and turn into Via del Proconsolo, past the Bargello, which was being built in Dante's time. Take Via dell'Anguillara until you come to Piazza Santa Croce. Outside Santa Croce there is a 19th-century statue of Dante. His sarcophagus, inside, is empty: Dante was buried in Ravenna.

INFORMATION

Distance 1km approx
Time 1 hour including visits
Start point ★ Baptistery
🚇 bIII
🚌 1, 6, 7, 11, 12, 14 (in the pedestrian zone)
End point Santa Croce
🚇 cIV
🚌 12, 14, 19, 23, 31, 32

| 0 | 200 m |
| 0 | 200 yards |

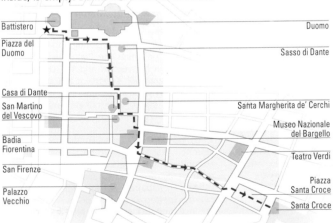

Battistero ★	Duomo
Piazza del Duomo	Sasso di Dante
Casa di Dante	
San Martino del Vescovo	Santa Margherita de' Cerchi
	Museo Nazionale del Bargello
Badia Fiorentina	Teatro Verdi
San Firenze	Piazza Santa Croce
Palazzo Vecchio	Santa Croce

Florence by Night

Left: *evening lights on the River Arno*
Centre: *the passeggiata on Via de Calzaiuoli*
Right: *a Florentine trattoria*

PICK OF THE PANORAMAS

The best evening vantage point has to be Piazzale Michelangelo (➤ 57), which gives a glorious panorama of the floodlit Duomo, Florence's twinkling lights and the misty hills beyond. The square draws the crowds during daylight hours but things are quieter at night. There's a restaurant and a couple of bars if you want to spend the evening here. It's best to avoid the park/gardens area below the square at night. In late June, the square hosts the spectacular firework display celebrating the feast of San Giovanni.

AN EVENING STROLL

To kick off the evening and for a taste of local life don't miss the *passeggiata*. Year-round, this quintessentially Italian nightly ritual sees the streets thronged with hundreds of locals, out to see and be seen, while window-shopping and meeting friends. The best place to see Florentine fashion peacocks in their finery is on Via dei Calzaiuoli, which links Piazza del Duomo with Piazza della Signoria. To enjoy a drink while you people-watch, head for Piazza della Repubblica, with its expensive cafés. After dinner, wander along the Lungarni, the name given to the streets beside the river. You'll inevitably be drawn to the Ponte Vecchio, as crowded in the evenings in summer as during the day.

FLOODLIT

Evening is the ideal time to admire Florentine architecture as the floodlighting enhances many buildings. Don't miss the Piazza della Signoria and the area between it and the Duomo. The private *palazzi* look superb at this time of day and you can peek into courtyards and loggias. Occasional street entertainers and itinerant traders add to the atmosphere.

CULTURE, CONCERTS AND CLUBBING

Florence has a year-round programme of cultural evening events (➤ 4). The free monthly tourist magazine *Chiavi d'Oro Toscana* has full listings. Newspapers are another good source. *Firenze Spettacolo* also details everything that's on, including rock concerts, clubs and discos.

FLORENCE's
top 25 sights

The sights are shown on the maps on the inside front cover and inside back cover, numbered **1** – **25** across the city

Cappella Brancacci

INFORMATION

- H7; Locator map A3
- Santa Maria del Carmine, Piazza del Carmine (enter through the cloisters)
- 055 238 2195
- Mon, Wed–Sat 10–5; Sun 1–5
- B
- Acceptable
- Moderate

Masaccio's Expulsion of Adam and Eve from Paradise

Part of the thrill of the Cappella Brancacci is the sensation that you are seeing the opening phases of the Renaissance, observing in Masaccio's frescos the power of expression and technical brilliance that inspired the Florentine painters of the 15th century.

The chapel   The Cappella Brancacci is a tiny chapel reached via the cloisters of the otherwise rather dull Santa Maria del Carmine. Two layers of frescos commissioned in 1424 by Felice Brancacci, a wealthy Florentine merchant and statesman, illustrate the life of St Peter, shown in his orange gown. The frescos were designed by Masolino da Panicale, who began painting them with his brilliant and promising pupil, Masaccio. In 1428 Masaccio took over from Masolino but died that year, aged 27, and the rest of the frescos were completed in the 1480s by Filippino Lippi.

Restoration   In the 1980s the chapel was superbly restored, with the removal of accumulated candlesoot and layers of an 18th-century egg-based gum (which had formed a mould). The frescos now have an intense radiance that makes it possible to see very clearly the shifts in emphasis between Masolino's work and that of Masaccio; contrast the serenity of Masolino's *Temptation of Adam and Eve* with the excruciating agony of Masaccio's *Expulsion of Adam and Eve from Paradise*. The restoration has also highlighted Masaccio's mastery of *chiaroscuro* (light and shade), which, combined with his grasp of perspective, was marvelled at and consciously copied by the 15th-century Florentine painters. His depiction of St Peter healing the sick (left of the altar as you face it, lower register) showed beggars and cripples with revolutionary realism.

Santa Maria Novella

The decorative marble façade of Tuscany's most important Gothic church incorporates billowing sails (emblem of Alberti's patron, Rucellai) and ostrich feathers (emblem of the Medici). Inside are immense artistic riches, donated by wealthy patrons.

Dominican Origins The church of Santa Maria Novella was built between 1279 and 1357 by Dominican monks. The lower part of the marble façade, Romanesque in style, is believed to have been executed by Fra Jacopo Talenti; the upper part was completed between 1456 and 1470 by Leon Battista Alberti.

Deceptive interior Inside, the church is vast and looks even longer than it is, thanks to the clever spacing of the columns. As you face the altar, on the left-hand side is a fresco of the *Trinità* (*c*1428) by Masaccio, one of the earliest paintings to demonstrate mastery of perspective. Many of the chapels in Santa Maria Novella are named after the church's wealthy patrons. The Strozzi Chapel (left transept) is dedicated to St Thomas Aquinas and decorated with frescos (1351–7) by Nardo di Cione depicting *Heaven and Hell*: Dante himself is represented in the *Last Judgment* just behind the altar. The Tornabuoni Chapel contains Ghirlandaio's fresco cycle of the life of St John the Baptist (1485) in contemporary costume.

The Dogs of God The Cappellone degli Spagnoli ('Spanish Chapel') was used by the courtiers of Eleanor of Toledo, wife of Cosimo I. In the frescos *Triumph of the Doctrine* (*c*1365) by Andrea da Firenze, the dogs of God (a pun on the word Dominican – *domini canes*) are sent to round up lost sheep into the fold of the church.

HIGHLIGHTS

- Marble façade
- Masaccio's *Trinità*
- Cappellone degli Spagnoli
- Tornabuoni Chapel

INFORMATION

- alII; Locator map B1
- Piazza di Santa Maria Novella
- Church 055 210 113. Museum 055 282 187
- Church Mon–Sat 7–noon, 3:30–6 (until 5 Sat); Sun 3:30–5. Closed during services. Museum Mon–Thu, Sat 9–2
- 5 minutes' walk from the railway station
- Good
- Church free. Museum moderate
  Duomo (➤ 37),
  Battistero (➤ 35),
  Campanile (➤ 36)

Palazzo Pitti

HIGHLIGHTS

- Frescoed ceilings by Pietro da Cortona, Galleria Palatina
- Raphael's *Madonna of the Chair* (c1516)
- Titian's overtly sexual *Mary Magdalene* (c1531)
- Van Dyck's *Charles I and Henrietta Maria* (c1632)
- Titian's *Portrait of a Gentleman* (1540)

Raphael's Madonna of the Chair

INFORMATION

- aIV; Locator map B3
- Piazza Pitti
- Galleria Palatina 055 238 8614. Museo degli Argenti 055 238 8710
- Galleria Palatina Tue–Sun 8:15–6:50. Museo degli Argenti Tue–Sun 8:15–1:50. Closed 1st, 3rd, 5th Mon of month, 2nd, 4th Sun
- B, C, 11, 36, 37
- Good
- Galleria Palatina expensive. Museo degli Argenti inexpensive

The Pitti Palace, with its four museums, is unremittingly grand, opulent and pompous. Its saving grace is the outstanding collection of Renaissance and baroque art in the Galleria Palatina.

Bigger and better The Palazzo Pitti was built in 1457 to designs by Filippo Brunelleschi for banker Luca Pitti. He wanted it to be bigger and better than the Medici Palace: the result has been likened to a 'rusticated Stalinist ministry'. Ironically, the Medici bought the Palazzo Pitti in 1550 when the Pitti lost their fortune, and it became the residence of the rulers of Florence.

Art The Galleria Palatina contains baroque and Renaissance works from the Medici collection as important as those in the Uffizi (► 40). Highlights include masterpieces by Titian, Raphael and Van Dyck displayed in a haphazard way that reflects the taste of the Medici, who had so many works of art that they didn't worry about hanging them in any order. The *Appartamenti Monumentali* (state rooms) are entered through the gallery.

Silver The Museo degli Argenti is a triumph of Medici wealth over taste. Rooms are full of ghoulish reliquaries, Roman glass and Roman and Byzantine vases in *pietra dura* style (inlaid with marble and semi-precious stone pieces) that belonged to Lorenzo the Magnificent. Upstairs is an attractive display of cameos, as well as a 17th-century coloured-glass Crucifixion scene that is in such appalling taste as to be hilarious.

Costume and Modern Art The Galleria del Costume reflects 18th- and 19th-century court fashions while the Galleria d'Arte Moderna shows Italian art from the late 19th to the early 20th centuries, not its greatest period.

Giardino di Boboli

The Boboli Gardens are, quite literally, a breath of fresh air: the only easily accessible reservoir of greenery and tranquillity in Florence, and a lovely retreat after a hard day's sightseeing.

Renaissance origins   The Boboli Gardens were created for the Medici when they moved to the Palazzo Pitti in 1550. They represent a superb example of Italian Renaissance gardening, an interplay between nature and artifice expressed in a geometrical arrangement of fountains, grass and low box hedges. In 1766 they were opened to the public, and in 1992 an (unpopular) entrance charge was imposed.

Amphitheatre   Just behind the Palazzo Pitti is the amphitheatre, built where the stone for the Palazzo Pitti was quarried. It was the site of the first-ever opera performance and is surrounded by maze-like alleys of fragrant, dusty bay trees. Go uphill past the Neptune Fountain (1565–68) to reach the Giardino dei Cavallieri, where roses and peonies wilt in the summer sun. The pretty building nearby houses the Porcelain Museum (no charge).

Island   The Viottolone, an avenue of cypresses planted in 1637 and studded with classical statues, leads to the *Isolotto*, an island set in a murky green pond dotted with pleasantly crumbling statues. In the centre is a copy of Giambologna's *Oceanus* fountain (1576), the original of which is in the Bargello (➤ 44).

Luxury garden shed   Do not miss *The Limonaia*, built in 1785 to protect rare citrus fruit trees from frost. Now it is a huge rococo garden shed, used for storing gardening equipment.

HIGHLIGHTS

● *Bacchus* fountain (1560)
● *La Grotta Grande*, a Mannerist cave-cum-sculpture gallery (1583–88)
● The *Kaffeehaus* café (1776, ➤ 70): superb views
● Views of the hills from the Giardino dei Cavallieri
● *Limonaia* (1785)
● The *Isolotto*

INFORMATION

✠ aIV; Locator map C3
✉ Piazza Pitti
☎ 055 265 1816/1838
🕐 Daily 8:15–one hour before sunset. Closed 1st and last Mon of month
🚌 B, C, 11, 36, 37
♿ Good
💷 Inexpensive
❓ Free maps at entrance

The Bacchus Fountain

Ponte Vecchio

No visit to Florence is complete without a saunter down this bridge; lined with old shops jutting precariously over the water, it is difficult to believe you're on a bridge and not just strolling down a narrow street.

HIGHLIGHTS

- Gold and jewellery shops
- Views of the Arno
- *Corridoio Vasariano* (1565)
- Bust of Cellini (1900)

INFORMATION

- ✚ bIV; Locator map C3
- ◉ Open all the time
- 🚍 In the pedestrian zone
- ♿ Good
- ↔ Uffizi (➤ 40), Palazzo Vecchio (➤ 43)

The test of time Near the Roman crossing, the Old Bridge was, until 1218, the only bridge across the Arno in Florence. The current bridge was rebuilt after a flood in 1345. During World War II it was the only bridge the fleeing Germans did not destroy; instead, they blocked access by demolishing the medieval buildings on either side. On 4 November 1966, the bridge miraculously withstood the tremendous weight of water and silt when the Arno burst its banks.

Private path When the Medici moved from the Palazzo Vecchio to the Palazzo Pitti, they decided they needed a connecting route from the Uffizi to the Palazzo Pitti on the other side of the river that enabled them to keep out of contact – heaven forbid! – with their people. The result was Vasari's *Corridoio Vasariano*, built in 1565 on top of the buildings lining the bridge's eastern parapet.

Shops Shops have been on the Ponte Vecchio since the 13th century: initially all types – butchers and fishmongers and later tanners, whose industrial waste caused a pretty rank stench. In 1593, Medici Duke Ferdinand I decreed that only goldsmiths and jewellers be allowed on the bridge, and in the centre stands the bust of the 16th-century goldsmith Cellini (1900). When the shops close at night, their wooden shutters make them look like suitcases. As one of the places that Florentines come to for the *passeggiata* (➤ 24), it also has a reputation for being where local drug dealers meet their clients.

Window-shopping on the Ponte Vecchio

Museo della Casa Fiorentina Antica

Unlike Florence's other museums, which abound in art, this restored 14th-century palace contains everyday items used by rich Florentines from the 14th to the 18th centuries, giving an intriguing insight into their lives.

A home to merchants The Palazzo Davanzati was built (*c*1330) for the Davizzi, who were wealthy wool merchants. From 1578 to 1904 it was owned by the Davanzati family who were also merchants. In 1904 it was restored to look like a 14th-century palace; in 1910 it was opened as a museum; and in 1951 it was acquired by the State. The palace is arranged around a courtyard.

Water on site A staircase links the courtyard to the Palazzo's three floors, and an elaborate system of pulleys transports water from the well, a great luxury in an age when most people had to collect their water by bucket from a public fountain. Pulleys were also used to transport goods to the kitchen, which was on the top floor so that, in the event of a kitchen fire, only the upper part of the palace would be burned.

The siege mentality Other signs of wealth are the sheer size and style of the building, which could be converted to a fortress in times of strife, famine or plague; supplies of grain, oil and other food would have been stored in the rooms off the courtyard. The façade has remained much as it was when it was first built, although the original battlements were replaced by a loggia, used for banquets and entertainments, in the 16th century. At the time of publication the sumptuous upper rooms are closed for restoration, but there is a temporary exhibition in the entrance hall displaying photographs of the museum's interior.

HIGHLIGHTS

- Sala dei Pappagalli (Parrot Room)
- Kitchen
- 17th-century shoe-shaped handwarmers
- Camera dei Pavoni (Peacock Room)

INFORMATION

- ✚ aIII; Locator map C2
- ✉ Palazzo Davanzati, Via Porta Rossa 13
- ☎ 055 238 8610
- 🕐 Tue–Sun 8:30–2. Closed alternate Sun and Mon. (At time of publication closed for restoration, but there is a temporary exhibition in the entrance hall)
- ♿ Details not available at time of publication, but likely to be part of the refurbishment
- 🚶 In the pedestrian zone
- 💷 Moderate
- ↔ Orsanmichele (➤ 39), Piazza della Signoria (➤ 42)

Cappelle Medicee

INFORMATION

- all; Locator map C1
- Piazza Madonna degli Aldobrandini
- 055 238 8602
- Daily 8:15–5; public hols 8:15–1:50 (last admission 30 minutes before closing). Closed 1st, 3rd, 5th Mon of month, 2nd, 4th Sun
- Pedestrian zone
- Poor
- Expensive
- Guided tours to see charcoal drawings

The tomb of Grand Duke Ferdinand

Of all the places in Florence associated with Michelangelo, the Medici Chapels, the mausoleum of the Medici family, are the most intriguing: here are his tomb sculptures, his *Madonna and Child* and even sketches.

Mausoleum The mausoleum of the Medici family is in three distinct parts of the church of San Lorenzo (▶ 33): the crypt, the Cappella dei Principi and the Sagrestia Nuova.

Crypt The crypt was where the bodies of minor members of the dynasty were unceremoniously dumped. Tidied up in the 19th century, it now houses numerous tomb slabs.

Chapel of the Princes In the Cappella dei Principi is a huge dome by Bernado Buontalenti, begun in 1604 and not completed until the 20th century. The inner surface is decorated in a heavy, grandiose way that speaks of political tyranny: the Medici coat of arms is rarely out of view. The tombs of six Medici Grand Dukes are in the chapel beneath the dome.

New Sacristy Right of the altar, the Sagrestia Nuova, built by Michelangelo between 1520 and 1534, is a reminder that the Medici were enlightened patrons. Michelangelo sculpted figures representing *Night* and *Day*, and *Dawn* and *Dusk* to adorn the tombs of Lorenzo, Duke of Urbino (1492–1519), and Giuliano, Duke of Nemours (1479–1516). The figure of *Night*, with moon, owl and mask, is one of his finest works. The *Madonna and Child* (1521) is also by Michelangelo. In a room left of the altar are charcoal drawings found in 1975 and attributed to Michelangelo.

San Lorenzo

San Lorenzo is the parish church and burial place of the Medici and is filled with art commissioned by them. Together with the Cappelle Medicee, it is a monument to the family's artistic patronage and dynastic grandeur.

A sacred site   San Lorenzo was rebuilt by Filippo Brunelleschi in 1419, on the site of one of the city's oldest churches (consecrated in AD 393). Its rough-hewn ochre exterior was to have been covered with a façade by Michelangelo: this was never added, but a model is in Casa Buonarroti (► 56). The most bizarre piece of art here is the statue of Anna Maria Luisa (*d*1743), the last of the Medici dynasty, found – like a displaced Limoges porcelain figure – outside the back of the church.

Airy interior   The church, with its *pietra serena* (grey sandstone) columns, is cool and airy. The bronze pulpits (*c*1460) depicting the Resurrection and scenes from the life of Christ are Donatello's last work. Savonarola (► 16, 17) preached his hellfire-and-brimstone sermons here. Bronzino's fresco (facing the altar, left) of the *Martyrdom of St Lawrence* (1569) is an absorbing Mannerist study of the human body in various contortions. Inside the geometrically precise and aesthetically pleasing Sagrestia Vecchia (Old Sacristy, 1421) are eight *tondi* (circular reliefs) by Donatello depicting the evangelists and scenes from the life of St John.

Biblioteca Laurenziana   The Laurentian Library houses the Medici's collection of manuscripts. This extraordinary example of Mannerist architecture by Michelangelo is left of the church, approached by a curvaceous *pietra serena* staircase via the cloisters. The readers' desks, which sit at a precipitous angle, are also by Michelangelo. The terracotta floor and wooden ceiling are by Tribolo.

HIGHLIGHTS

- Biblioteca Laurenziana (begun 1524)
- Staircase by Michelangelo
- Bronzino's *Martyrdom of St Lawrence*
- Pulpits by Donatello
- Brunelleschi's Sagrestia Vecchia

INFORMATION

- ✚ bII; Locator map C1
- ✉ Piazza San Lorenzo
- ☎ 055 216 634. Library 055 230 2991
- ◷ Daily 7–noon, 3:30–6:30. Closed during services. Library Mon–Sat 9–1
- ▣ In the pedestrian zone
- ♿ Poor
- ◉ Free
- ⬌ Cappelle Medicee (► 32), Duomo (► 37), Battistero (► 35), Palazzo Medici-Riccardi (► 34)

Market stalls outside San Lorenzo

Palazzo Medici-Riccardi

HIGHLIGHTS

- Gozzoli's fresco cycle of the *Journey of the Magi* (1459–63)

INFORMATION

- ✚ bII; Locator map C1
- ✉ Via Cavour 3
- ☎ 055 276 0340
- 🕐 Thu–Tue 9–7
- 🚌 1, 6, 7
- ♿ Good
- 🏛 Cappella dei Magi moderate
- ⟷ San Lorenzo (➤ 33)
- ❓ The Palazzo houses the Museo Mediceo, used for temporary exhibitions

The Medici ruled with a mixture of tyranny and humanity. This is reflected in the imposing façade of their head-quarters, with its fearsome lattice of window bars and incongruous built-in bench at seat height, where passers-by could, and still can, sit and relax.

Medici origins The Palazzo Medici-Riccardi, now mostly government offices, was the seat of the Medici family from its completion in 1444 until 1540, when Cosimo I moved the Medici residence to the Palazzo Vecchio and this palace was bought by the Riccardi family.

Setting a trend The palace, designed by Michelozzo, was widely imitated in Florence, for example in the Palazzo Strozzi and the Palazzo Pitti. It is characterised by huge slabs of stone, rusticated to give a roughly hewn rural appearance. The courtyard is in a lighter style, with a graceful colonnade and black and white sgraffito decoration of medallions, based on the designs of Roman intaglios collected by the Medici and displayed in the Museo degli Argenti (➤ 28).

Detail from Gozzoli's 15th-century fresco, Journey of the Magi

A regal scene Steps right of the entrance lead to the Cappella dei Magi. This tiny chapel has the dazzling fresco cycle depicting the *Journey of the Magi* (1459–63) that Piero de' Medici commissioned from Gozzoli in honour of the Compagnia dei Magi, a religious organisation to which the Medici belonged. Portraits of the Medici are believed to have been incorporated into the cast of characters, while the procession recalls the pageantry of the Compagnia dei Magi and includes enchanting animals: leopards, monkeys and a falcon whose claws pierce the entrails of a hare.

Battistero

Perhaps the most loved of all Florence's edifices is the Baptistery, referred to by Dante as his 'bel San Giovanni', and dedicated to St John the Baptist, the city's patron saint. With its octagonal, marble exterior and bronze doors, it is a beautiful building.

Roman origins The Baptistery is one of the oldest buildings in Florence: the remains of a Roman palace lie under it, and the dates given for the present construction vary between the 5th and the 7th centuries AD. For much of Florence's history it was the place where all Florentines were baptised and, inside, it is clear where the font stood until its removal in 1576.

Rich ornament The entire outer surface is covered with a beautiful design of white and green marble, added between the 11th and 13th centuries. Inside, the ceiling is encrusted with stunning mosaics: above the altar, designs show the Virgin and St John the Baptist; the main design shows the Last Judgement, with the sinful being devoured by diabolical creatures, while the virtuous ascend to heaven. Do not miss the tessellated floor, almost Islamic in its intricate geometry.

Bronze doors The Baptistery is renowned, above all, for its bronze doors: the south doors, by Pisano (1336), and Ghiberti's north and east doors (1403–24 and 1425–52). The east doors, referred to by Michelangelo as the 'Gates of Paradise', are divided into 10 panels depicting Old Testament scenes, using Renaissance techniques such as linear perspective. The originals are in the Museo dell'Opera del Duomo (➤ 38); the copies were funded by Japanese patronage.

HIGHLIGHTS

- 13th-century mosaics of the Last Judgement
- Ghiberti's east doors
- Pisano's south doors
- Zodiac pavement
- Romanesque marble exterior

Exterior of the Battistero

INFORMATION

- ✚ bIII; Locator map C2
- ✉ Piazza San Giovanni
- ☎ 055 230 2885
- 🕐 Mon–Sat 12–6:30; Sun 8:30–1:30
- 🚌 1, 6, 7, 11, 14, 23 (in the pedestrian zone)
- ♿ Good
- 💶 Inexpensive
- ↔ Duomo (➤ 37), Campanile (➤ 36)

35

Campanile

HIGHLIGHTS

- Views from the top
- Reliefs by Pisano and della Robbia

INFORMATION

- bIII; Locator map C2
- Piazza del Duomo
- 055 271 071/230 2885
- Apr–Sep: daily 8:30–7:30. Oct–Mar: daily 9–5:30 (last admission 40 minutes before closing)
- In the pedestrian zone
- Impossible
- Moderate
- Duomo (➤ 37), Battistero (➤ 35)

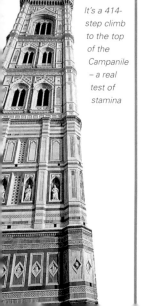

It's a 414-step climb to the top of the Campanile – a real test of stamina

Tall, graceful and beautifully proportioned, the bell tower of the Duomo is one of the loveliest in Italy and adds a calm and graceful note to the otherwise busy cathedral complex.

Multiple effort The Campanile, or bell tower, of the Duomo stands 85m, just 6m lower than the Duomo. It was begun in 1334 and completed in 1359. Giotto was involved in its design, but by the time of his death in 1337 only the base had been completed. Andrea Pisano completed the second storey and the tower was finished by Francesco Talenti.

Relief sculpture The outer surface is decorated in the same polychrome marble as the Duomo: white marble from Carrara, green marble from Prato and pink marble from the Maremma – the flat marshland area along the coast of southern Tuscany. Around the bottom are two sets of relief sculptures: the lower tier are in hexagonal panels, the upper tier in diamonds. What you see are in fact copies; the originals have been moved to the Museo dell'Opera del Duomo (➤ 38) to prevent further atmospheric damage. The reliefs in the hexagonal panels, which were executed by Pisano (although some are believed to have been designed by Giotto), show the Creation of Man, the Arts and the Industries, including weaving, hunting and navigation. On the north face the five Liberal Arts (grammar, philosophy, music, arithmetic and astrology) were executed by Luca della Robbia. The upper tier of reliefs, also the work of Pisano, illustrate the Seven Planets, the Seven Virtues and the Liberal Arts; while the Seven Sacraments have been attributed to Alberto Arnoldi.

Duomo

The famous dome of this cathedral dominates the Florence skyline, with its eight white ribs on a background of terracotta tiles. From close up, the size of the building is overwhelming.

A lengthy building project The cathedral of Santa Maria del Fiori, the Florence Duomo, is a vast Gothic structure built on the site of the 7th-century church of Santa Reparata, whose remains can be seen in the crypt. It was built at the end of the 13th century, although the colossal dome, which dominates the exterior, was not added until the 15th century, and the façade was not finished until the 19th century. The exterior is a decorative riot of pink, white and green marble; the interior is stark and plain. The clock above the entrance on the west wall inside was designed in 1443 by Paolo Uccello in accordance with the *ora italica*, according to which the 24th hour of the day ends at sunset.

Roman influences Built by Filippo Brunelleschi, who won the competition for its commission in 1418, the dome is egg-shaped and was made without scaffolding. Its herringbone brickwork was copied from the Pantheon in Rome. The best way to see the dome is to climb its 463 steps: the route takes you through the interior, where you can see Vasari's much-reviled frescos of the Last Judgement (1572–9), and towards the lantern, from which the views are fantastic.

Explosion of the cart At Easter the *Scoppio del Carro*, a Mass-cum-theatrical pageant, culminates in a mechanical dove being launched from the altar along a wire to the entrance, so that at noon its beak ignites a cart full of fireworks outside the Duomo doors.

HIGHLIGHTS

- Brunelleschi's dome
- Santa Reparata remains
- Uccello's mural to a 14th-century Captain-General

Detail from one of the Duomo's doors

INFORMATION

- ✝ bIII; Locator map C2
- ✉ Piazza del Duomo
- ☎ 055 271 071/230 2885
- 🕐 Cathedral Mon–Sat 10–5; Sun 1:30–5. 1st Sat of the month 10–3:30.
  Dome (access from south side of cathedral in Piazza del Duomo) Mon–Fri 8:30–7, Sat 8:30–5 (until 3:20 first Sat of month)
- 🚌 1, 6, 7, 11, 14 (in the pedestrian zone)
- ♿ Good (access via the entrance for the dome)
- 💷 Free. Dome moderate
- ↔ Campanile (► 36), Battistero (► 35)

Museo dell'Opera del Duomo

HIGHLIGHTS

- Choir lofts
- Original panels from the Campanile
- Michelangelo's *Pietà*
- Original panels from the 'Gates of Paradise'
- Donatello's *Maddalena*

INFORMATION

- bIII; Locator map D2
- Piazza del Duomo 9
- 055 230 2885
- Mon–Sat 9:30–6:30; Sun 8–2
- In the pedestrian zone
- Poor
- Moderate
- Duomo (➤ 37), Campanile (➤ 36), Battistero (➤ 35)

Detail from della Robbia's choir loft

There is something very pleasing about the idea of visiting the Cathedral Workshop, the maintenance section of the huge artistic undertaking that the cathedral complex represents.

Refuge from pollution This workshop-museum was founded when the Duomo was built, to maintain the art of the cathedral. Its location was chosen in the 15th century, and it was in its courtyard that Michelangelo sculpted his *David*. Since 1891, it has housed works removed from the cathedral complex: indeed, one reason why the Duomo seems so empty is that so much is now exhibited in the Museo dell'Opera del Duomo. It is also a refuge for outdoor sculptures.

Michelangelo's *Pietà* On the mezzanine levels you can see the construction materials and instruments used for Brunelleschi's dome, such as pulleys, buckets and brick moulds. On the main landing is the *Pietà* (begun *c*1550) by Michelangelo, which used to be in the Duomo. It is believed he intended it for his own tomb; the hooded figure of Nicodemus is often interpreted as a self-portrait. The damage to Christ's left leg and arm is believed to have been inflicted by Michelangelo in frustration at his failing skills.

Artists compared The main room on the first floor contains two choir lofts that once stood in the Duomo: one by Luca della Robbia (1431–8), the other by Donatello (1433–9). This is an opportunity to compare two great Renaissance artists: della Robbia's infants are smooth, their movements lyrical; Donatello's convey more vigour. In the room on the left are reliefs by Pisano from the Campanile (➤ 36); in the final ground-floor room Ghiberti's original 'Gates of Paradise' are displayed as their restoration is completed.

Orsanmichele

Here, perhaps more than anywhere else in Florence, you are made aware of the guilds that were so influential in the city's history. Their emblems and patron saints adorn this building.

Vegetable garden Orsanmichele gets its name from the fact that it was surrounded by the *orto* (vegetable garden) of a Benedictine monastery when it was first built around AD 750 as the oratory of St Michael. The present building was constructed in 1336 as a market and grain store; by 1380 the ground floor had become a church.

Saintly sculptures In 1339 it was decided that each of the major tradesmen's guilds should provide a statue of their respective patron saint to stand outside. By happy accident, nothing was completed until the Renaissance was in full swing in the 15th century, so the commissions were executed by artists of the calibre of Verrocchio, Ghiberti, Donatello and Luca della Robbia. Most of the niches for the saints are now empty or filled with copies. Many of the sculptures have been moved to Florentine museums such as the Bargello (➤ 44).

Tabernacle Inside Orsanmichele is gloomy. The walls reveal patchy traces of frescos; these, too, depict the various guild patron saints. The central feature, however, is the tabernacle (1348–59) by Orcagna, which frames the exquisite *Madonna and Child* (1347) by Bernardo Daddi. To properly appreciate the architecture of Orsanmichele it is best to visit the museum (although at the time of publication this is closed for restoration). Here you get a true impression of the immense size of the building, and the views are spectacular (➤ 57).

HIGHLIGHTS

- Bernardo Daddi's *Madonna and Child*
- Orcagna's tabernacle
- della Robbia's roundels
- Museo di Orsanmichele

INFORMATION

- bIII; Locator map C2
- Via dei Calzaiuoli
- 055 284 944
- Mon–Fri 9–12, 4–6; Sat 9–1, 4–6; Sun 9–1, 4–6. Closed 1st and last Mon of month and during services. Museum currently closed for restoration
- In the pedestrian zone
- Good (except museum)
- Free
- Piazza della Signoria (➤ 42), Palazzo Vecchio (➤ 43)

Bernardo Daddi's Madonna and Child

Galleria degli Uffizi

INFORMATION

- bIV; Locator map C3
- Loggiato degli Uffizi 6
- 055 238 8651. (Book ahead to avoid queues by calling 055 294 833)
- Tue–Sun 8:15–6:50 (last admission 45 minutes before closing). Closed 1 May
- In the pedestrian zone
- Good
- Expensive
- Palazzo Vecchio (➤ 43), Ponte Vecchio (➤ 30), Piazza della Signoria (➤ 42)

The **Uffizi encompasses the artistic developments of the Renaissance and beyond. It is a powerful expression of Florence's extraordinary role in the history of art.**

Medici art The gallery contains part of the Medici's art collection, bequeathed in 1737 by Anna Maria Luisa. The building was designed by Vasari, in the 1560s, as the administrative offices (*uffizi*) of the Grand Duchy. Parts of the building and collection that were damaged by the 1993 bomb were restored and reopened in 1998.

From sculpture to painting Today people come for the paintings, but until the 19th century the attraction was sculpture (mostly now in the Bargello, ➤ 44). The collection is displayed in chronological order, starting with the first stirrings of the Renaissance in the 13th century and ending with works by Caravaggio, Rembrandt and Canaletto from the 17th and 18th centuries. Uccello's *Battle of San Romano* (1456) exemplifies the technical advances of the Renaissance, such as the mastery of linear perspective, while Filippo Lippi's *Madonna and Child with Two Angels* (c1465) reveals the emotional focus typical of the period.

Medici Venus Perhaps most fascinating is the Tribune, an octagonal chamber with a mother-of-pearl ceiling. In the centre is the Medici *Venus* (a copy of Praxiteles' Aphrodite of Cnidos, c350 BC), whose sensuous derrière earned her the reputation of the sexiest sculpture of the ancient world. Portraits include Bronzino's *Giovanni de Medici* (c1545), a smiling boy holding a goldfinch.

Early birds Go early in the morning or in the late afternoon to avoid the queues. The café has superb views of Piazza della Signoria.

Above: Botticelli's Birth of Venus *(1485)*

Museo di Storia della Scienza

Here you'll find a fascinating collection of scientific instruments, a reminder that the Florentine Renaissance was not only an artistic movement, but also fostered the origins of modern science.

Physics and natural sciences Located in the 14th-century Palazzo Castellani, the Museum of the History of Science houses a well-organised collection which in large part belonged to the Medici Grand Dukes. In 1775 the Museum of Physics and Natural Sciences was opened and in 1929 the collection was moved to its current location. The galleries are on the first and second floors; the ground floor is the library of the Istituto di Storia della Scienza.

Galileo Galilei There is a sizeable exhibition devoted to Galileo (1564–1642), Pisa-born but adopted by the Medici as the court mathematician. Some exhibits border on the hagiographic: not only is his telescope displayed, but also the middle finger of his right hand, preserved in a reliquary.

Maps and planets The map room has a 16th-century map of the world by the Portuguese cartographer Lopo Homem, revealing the limit of European geographical knowledge at that time: Australasia is nowhere to be found and the tip of South America fades into blankness. It also has a collection of armillary spheres, used to divine the movements of the planets.

Obstetric models On the second floor is a series of 18th-century wax and ceramic models of birth deformities, complete with helpful hints for the doctor, such as where to insert the forceps.

HIGHLIGHTS

- Galileo's telescope
- Lopo Homem's map of the world (16th century)
- Antonio Santucci's armillary sphere (1573)
- Copy of Lorenzo della Volpaia's clock of the planets (1593)
- 18th-century models of birth deformities

INFORMATION

- bIV; Locator map C3
- Piazza dei Guidici 1
- 055 239 8876
- Mon, Wed, Thur, Fri 9:30–5; Tue, Sat 9:30–1 (also 2nd Sun of month 10–1, Oct–May)
- 23
- Excellent
- Expensive
- Excellent guide book

Above: a sketch of Galileo's telescope
Top: 16th-century sundials

Piazza della Signoria

HIGHLIGHTS

- Loggia dei Lanzi (1376)
- Cellini's *Perseus* (1554)
- Giambologna's *Rape of the Sabine Women* (1583)
- Ammannati's *Neptune* (1575)
- Rivoire café
- Sorbi newspaper and postcard kiosk

INFORMATION

- ✚ bIII: Locator map C2
- ✉ Piazza della Signoria
- ▣ In the pedestrian zone
- ♿ Good
- ↔ Palazzo Vecchio (➤ 43), Galleria degli Uffizi (➤ 40)

Sculpture of Neptune *by Ammannati*

Standing in the Piazza della Signoria in the shadow of the grim, forbidding Palazzo Vecchio, it is impossible to escape the sense of Florence's past political might.

Political piazza The Piazza della Signoria has been the centre of political life in Florence since the 14th century. It was the scene of great triumphs, such as the return of the Medici in 1530, but also of the Bonfire of the Vanities instigated by Savonarola (➤ 16, 17), who was himself burned at the stake here in 1498, denounced as a heretic by the Inquisition.

Significant sculptures The sculptures here bristle with political connotations, many of them fiercely contradictory. Michelangelo's *David* (the original is in the Accademia) was placed outside the Palazzo Vecchio as a symbol of the Republic's defiance of the tyrannical Medici. The *Neptune* (1575), by Ammannati, celebrates the Medici's maritime ambitions, and Giambologna's statue of Duke *Cosimo I* (1595) is an elegant portrait of the man who brought all of Tuscany under Medici military rule. The statue of *Perseus* holding Medusa's head, by Cellini (1554), is a stark reminder of what happened to those who crossed the Medici.

Loggia dei Lanzi The graceful Loggia dei Lanzi, which functions as an open-air sculpture gallery, was designed by Orcagna in 1376; its curved arches foretell Renaissance classicism.

Postcard paradise Sorbi, the newspaper kiosk, has an unrivalled collection of postcards and newspapers which you could enjoy over a drink in the Rivoire café (➤ 70).

Palazzo Vecchio

With its fortress-like castellations and its commanding 95m bell tower, the Palazzo Vecchio conveys a message of political power supported by military strength.

HIGHLIGHTS

● Sala delle Carte
● Sala dei Gigli
● Michelangelo's *Victory*
● Donatello's *Judith and Holofernes*
● View from the Terrazza di Saturno
● Salone dei Cinquecento

Town Hall The Palazzo Vecchio is still Florence's town hall, as it has been since its completion by Arnolfo di Cambio in 1302. It was substantially remodelled for Duke Cosimo I, who made it his palace in 1540. It became known as the Palazzo Vecchio (Old Palace) when Cosimo transferred his court to the Palazzo Pitti. During the brief period when Florence was the capital of Italy (1865–71), it housed the Parliament and Foreign Ministry.

Assembly room The vast Salone dei Cinquecento (53.5m by 22m; 18m high) was designed in the 1490s, during the era of the Florentine Republic, as the meeting place of the 500-strong ruling assembly. Vasari painted the military scenes of Florence's victory over Siena and Pisa (1563–65). The theme of Florence's might is further underscored by the presence of Michelangelo's *Victory* (1533–34), as well as sculptures of the *Labours of Hercules* by Vincenzo dei Rossi. The ceiling is painted with the *Apotheosis of Cosimo I* (also by Vasari), lest we miss the point.

Loggia views On the second floor the Terrazza di Saturno is an open loggia with views to the hills. The Sala dei Gigli is decorated with gold fleurs-de-lys (symbol of Florence) and houses Donatello's *Judith and Holofernes* (1456–60). The most interesting room is last: the Sala delle Carte (Map Room), with its wonderful collection of globes and 57 maps painted on leather, showing the world as it was known in 1563.

INFORMATION

✚ bIV; Locator map C2
✉ Piazza della Signoria
☎ 055 276 8465
◷ Mon–Wed, Fri, Sat 9–7; Thu, Sun 9–2. Mon, Fri in summer late opening
🚌 19, 23, 31, 32
♿ Good
💶 Expensive
🔄 Gallerie degli Uffizi (► 40)
❓ In summer, walks along the parapets and other parts of the Palazzo Vecchio not usually open to the public are arranged. Details from the tourist information centre

Bargello

The Bargello, with its airy courtyard, is so pleasant that you would want to visit it even if it were not home to what is arguably the finest collection of Renaissance sculpture in the world.

Law court, prison and museum   Built in 1255, the Bargello was the first seat of Florence's city government and served as the city's main law court before being passed to the *Bargello* (Chief of Police) in 1574; it was used as a prison until 1859. In 1865 it opened as a museum, with an unrivalled collection of Renaissance sculpture and decorative arts.

Courtyard art   The courtyard walls, once the site of executions, carry the coats of arms of the Podestà (chief magistrates), whose headquarters were here, and 16th-century sculpture, including Giambologna's *Oceanus* from the Boboli Gardens (► 29). The ground floor has works by Michelangelo (► 56), Cellini and Giambologna, including *Mercury* (1564).

The Salone del Consiglio Generale, which once served as a courtroom

David and St George   In the Salone del Consiglio Generale, a vaulted hall on the first floor that was once the courtroom, works by Donatello include his decidedly camp bronze *David* (*c*1430–40), dressed in long boots and a jaunty hat (the first freestanding nude since the Roman period), and his *St George* (1416), sculpted for the exterior of Orsanmichele (► 39).

Terracottas, medals and bronzes   On the second floor enamelled terracottas by the della Robbia family include the bust of a boy by Andrea della Robbia. There are also displays of Italian medals and small Renaissance bronzes. The arms room has ivory-inlay saddles, guns and armour.

Galleria dell'Accademia

Michelangelo's *David*, exhibited in the Accademia, has a powerful impact: the intensity of his gaze, that assured posture, those huge hands, the anatomical precision of the veins and the muscles.

Art school The Accademia was founded in 1784 to teach techniques of painting, drawing and sculpture. Since 1873 it has housed the world's single most important collection of sculptures by Michelangelo. There are also sculptures by other artists, as well as many paintings, mostly from the Renaissance period.

Michelangelo's masterpiece The principal attraction is the *David* by Michelangelo, sculpted in 1504 and exhibited outside the Palazzo Vecchio until 1873, when it was transferred to the Accademia to protect it from environmental damage. It captures the moment at which the young David contemplates defying the giant Goliath. The pose is classical, determined by the thin dimensions of Carrara marble slab.

Freedom from stone The *Prisoners* (1505) were made for the tomb of Pope Julius II. The title refers to Michelangelo's belief that when he sculpted a statue, he was freeing the figure from the marble, and the style, particularly favoured by Michelangelo, was called the *non finito* (unfinished). After his death, the *Prisoners* were moved to the Grotta Grande in the Boboli Gardens (➤ 29), where the originals were replaced with casts in 1908. Among the other sculptures is the original plaster model for *The Rape of the Sabine Women* (1583), Giambologna's last work; the marble version is in the Loggia dei Lanzi in Piazza della Signoria (➤ 42).

HIGHLIGHTS

- Michelangelo's *David*
- Michelangelo's *Prisoners*
- Giambologna's *Rape of the Sabine Women*
- Buonaguida's *Tree of Life*

INFORMATION

- ✚ bII; Locator map D1
- ✉ Via Ricasoli 60
- ☎ 055 238 8609
- 🕐 Tue–Sun 8:15–6:50. Closed 1 May
- 🚇 San Marco
- ♿ Good
- 💷 Expensive
- ↔ San Marco (➤ 46), Santissima Annunziata (➤ 47)

Michelangelo's David

San Marco

INFORMATION

- ➕ bII; Locator map D1
- ✉ Piazza San Marco 1
- ☎ 055 238 8608
- 🕐 Tue–Fri 8:15–1:50; Sat 8:15–6:50; Sun 8:15–1:50 (last admission 30 min before closing). Closed 1st, 3rd, 5th Sun, 2nd, 4th Mon of the month
- 🚌 1, 6, 7, 10, 11, 17, 20, 25, 31, 32, 33
- ♿ Good
- 🎫 Moderate

The Annunciation *(1442), Fra Angelico*

Dominated by the lovely paintings of Fra Angelico, the soothing convent of San Marco has an aura of monastic calm that is conducive to appreciating the religious themes depicted.

Medici motives San Marco was founded in the 13th century by Silvestrine monks. In 1437 Cosimo il Vecchio invited the Dominican monks of Fiesole to move into the convent and had it rebuilt by Michelozzo, a gesture motivated by his guilt for having made so much money from banking (which was not theologically correct) and also by the fact that the Dominicans were useful allies. Ironically, Savonarola (➤ 16, 17), who denounced the decadence of the Medici at the end of the 15th century, came to prominence as the Dominican prior of San Marco.

A feast for the eyes The Chiostro di Sant' Antonino, the cloister through which you enter, is decorated with faded frescos by Fra Angelico and other Florentine artists. In the Ospizio dei Pellegrini, where pilgrims were cared for, there is a superb collection of freestanding paintings by Fra Angelico and his followers. At the top of the staircase on the way to the dormitory is Fra Angelico's *Annunciation* (1440), an image of great tenderness and grace. Each of the 44 monks' cells is adorned with a small fresco by Fra Angelico or one of his assistants. The themes include the *Entombment* (cell 2) and the *Mocking of Christ* (cell 7). Savonarola's rooms house an exhibition about him. Cells 38 and 39 were reserved for Cosimo il Vecchio, who periodically spent time in the monastery.

The first public library The library, also on the first floor, built in 1441 by Michelozzo, was the first public library in Europe.

Santissima Annunziata

The intimacy and delicate architecture of the Piazza della Santissima contrast with the grandeur of much of Florence. The roundels of babies on the Spedale degli Innocenti are quite enchanting.

Old New Year The Feast of the Annunciation on 25 March used to be New Year in the old Florentine calendar, and for that reason the church and the square have always played a special role in the life of the city. Every year, on 25 March, a fair is still held in the square and special biscuits called *brigidini* are sold. The square is central but off the beaten tourist track.

Wedding flowers The church of Santissima Annunziata was built by Michelozzo in 1444–81 on the site of a Servite oratory. Entry is through an atrium known as the Chiostrino dei Voti (1447), which has the air of a rickety green-house though the frescos inside are superb. They include Rosso Fiorentino's *Assumption*, Pontormo's *Visitation* and Andrea del Sarto's *Birth of the Virgin*. For some Florentines, the star attraction is a fresco of the Virgin Mary (said to have been started by a monk in 1252 and finished by an angel, to which newlyweds present the wedding bouquet to ensure a happy marriage.

Early orphanage The Spedale degli Innocenti, on the east side of the piazza, was the first orphanage in Europe; part of the building is still used for the purpose, and UNICEF has offices here. Designed by Filippo Brunelleschi in 1419, it is decorated with enamelled terracotta roundels by della Robbia showing babies in swaddling clothes (1498).

HIGHLIGHTS

● Andrea della Robbia's roundels
● Façade of the Spedale degli Innocenti
● Rosso Fiorentino's *Assumption*
● Pontormo's *Visitation*
● Andrea del Sarto's *Birth of the Virgin*

INFORMATION

✚ cII; Locator map D1
✉ Piazza della Santissima Annunziata
☎ 055 239 8034. Spedale degli Innocenti 055 234 9317
🕐 Daily 7:30–12:30, 4–6:30. Closed during services. Spedale: Mon, Tue, Thu–Sat 8:30–2; Sun 8–1
🚌 6, 31, 32
♿ Good
🎫 Inexpensive to Spedale

Andrea del Sarto's work in the Chiostrino

Cappella dei Pazzi

HIGHLIGHTS

- Cappella dei Pazzi
- Cloister
- Roundels of the evangelists
- Cimabue's crucifix (13th century)
- Taddeo Gaddi's fresco (1333)
- Donatello's *St Louis of Toulouse* (1424)

INFORMATION

- cIV; Locator map E3
- Piazza Santa Croce
- 055 244 619
- Apr–Oct: Thu–Tue 10–7. Nov–Mar: Thu–Tue 10–6
- 23, 13, B
- Good
- Inexpensive
- Santa Croce (➤ 49)

In contrast to the adjacent church of Santa Croce, a key stop on the tourist circuit, the cloisters are not much visited. The solitude is perfect for appreciating their grace and harmony.

Convent building   On the south side of Santa Croce are the buildings of a former convent. These include the Cappella dei Pazzi, one of the great architectural masterpieces of the early Renaissance, and a 14th-century refectory, which houses the Museo dell'Opera di Santa Croce. This is one of the lowest areas in Florence, and to the left of the Cappella dei Pazzi a plaque almost 6m up shows the high point of the November 1966 floodwaters. The second cloister, a haven of calm, was designed by Filippo Brunelleschi.

The Pazzi Chapel   The Cappella dei Pazzi, which was commissioned as a chapter house by Andrea dei Pazzi and designed by Brunelleschi (*c*1430), is incorporated into the cloisters. Inside, this graceful domed chapel is done in grey *pietra serena* against a plain white plaster background, embellished only by enamelled terracotta roundels: 12 roundels by Luca della Robbia show the Apostles, with four more of the evangelists, attributed to Brunelleschi or Donatello, around the dome.

Museum   The museum is small but contains many important works, including a restored crucifix by Giovanni Cimabue, almost destroyed in the 1966 floods. On the walls a huge fresco by Taddeo Gaddi shows the Last Supper, the Tree of Life, St Louis of Toulouse, St Francis, St Benedict and Mary Magdalene washing Christ's feet. It is hard to miss the gilded bronze statue of *St Louis of Toulouse* (1424), sculpted by Donatello for the Orsanmichele (➤ 39).

Roundel of St Luke, one of the four evangelists

Santa Croce

Despite its vast size and swarms of tourists, Santa Croce is touchingly intimate, perhaps because of the sense that one somehow knows the people buried here.

Florentine favourite Santa Croce, rebuilt for the Franciscan order in 1294 by Arnolfo di Cambio, is the burial place of the great and the good in Florence.

Civic pantheon Michelangelo is buried in Santa Croce, as are Rossini, Machiavelli and the Pisa-born Galileo Galilei, who was excommunicated during the Inquisition and was not allowed a Christian burial until 1737 – 95 years after his death. There is also a memorial to Dante (▶ 17), whose sarcophagus is empty.

English connections The church exterior is covered with a polychrome marble façade added in 1863 and paid for by the English benefactor Sir Francis Sloane. It looks over the Piazza Santa Croce, site of an annual football game in medieval costume (▶ 85).

Artistic riches The artistic wealth in Santa Croce is stunning; frescos by Gaddi (1380) in the Cappella Maggiore tell the story of the holy cross ('Santa Croce') and beautiful frescos by Giotto in the Bardi and Peruzzi chapels show scenes from the lives of St Francis and St John the Evangelist. An unusual relief *Annunciation* in gilded limestone by Donatello decorates the south nave's wall. Don't miss the memorial to 19th-century playwright Giovanni Battista Nicolini, left of the entrance facing the altar, said to have inspired the *Statue of Liberty*. Santa Croce was severely hit by flooding in 1966, and a tide mark shows far up on the pillars and walls.

HIGHLIGHTS

- Giotto's frescos (1320–25)
- Tombs of Michelangelo, Machiavelli, Galileo
- Painted wooden ceiling
- Donatello's *Annunciation* (1435)
- Polychrome marble façade (1863)

INFORMATION

- clV; Locator map E3
- Piazza Santa Croce
- 055 244 619
- Apr–Oct: Mon–Sat 9:30–5:30; Sun 3–5.30. Nov–Mar: Mon–Sat 8–12:30, 3–5:30; Sun 3–5.30. Closed during services
- 23, 13, B
- Acceptable
- Free

The vast interior of Santa Croce

San Miniato al Monte

INFORMATION

- J8; Locator map E4
- Off Viale Galileo Galilei
- 055 234 2768
- Apr–Oct: daily 8–12, 4–7. Nov–Mar: daily 8–12, 2:30–6. Closed during services
- 12, 13
- Good
- Free

Michelozzo's free-standing chapel

San Miniato is a wonderful sight on the hill above Florence, its marble façade glistening in the sunlight. Close up it is even more appealing, a jewel of the Romanesque inside and outside.

Christian martyr   San Miniato (St Minias) was an early Christian martyr who came to Florence from the Levant in the 3rd century and was martyred in the Roman amphitheatre that stood on the site of today's Piazza della Signoria, by order of the Emperor Decius. It is said that his decapitated body picked up his head and walked into the hills. His shrine, the site of the present church, was built where he finally collapsed. The church was initially run by Benedictine monks, then by Cluniacs, and finally, from 1373 to the present day, by the Olivetans. In the Benedictine shop on the right as you exit, monks sell honey and herbal potions as well as Coca-Cola.

An eagle visitation   The church was built in 1018, with a green and white marble façade, typical of the Tuscan Romanesque, added at the end of the 11th century and mosaics in the 13th century. On the pinnacle of the church a gilded copper statue of an eagle carries a bale of cloth (1410): this is the symbol of the Arte di Calimala, the wool importers' guild, which supported the church in the Middle Ages.

Miraculous crucifix   Inside, a lovely inlaid floor (*c*1207) incorporates zodiac and animal themes. The capitals of the columns are Roman and Byzantine, and the wooden ceiling, restored in the 19th century, dates from 1322. The mosaics in the apse (1297) show the Virgin and St Minias. In the nave is a chapel (1448) by Michelozzo, built to house a miraculous crucifix that is now in Santa Trinita (➤ 55).

FLORENCE's
best

Museums & Galleries

JOINT TICKET

If you are on a serious culture trip, buy a carnet, which gives discounts on tickets to a number of Florentine museums, including the Museo Bardini, the Museo di Santa Maria Novella (➤ 27), the Palazzo Vecchio (➤ 43), the Museo di 'Firenze Com'era', Museo Stibbert and Museo Marino Marini. The carnet can be bought from any of the participating museums.

MUSEO ARCHEOLOGICO

One of the best places to see Etruscan art. There are also Roman, Greek and Egyptian exhibits.

✚ cII ✉ Palazzo della Crocetta, Via della Colonna 36 ☎ 055 23575 🕐 Mon 2–7; Tue, Thu 8:30–7; Wed, Fri–Sun 8:30–2 🚌 6 ♿ Good 💲 Moderate

MUSEO BARDINI

Stefano Bardini was a 19th-century art dealer with a knack of acquiring choice pieces at knock-down prices. He made some particularly judicious purchases in the field of church architecture, some of which are worked into the fabric of the *palazzo*, such as door frames and the wooden ceiling in room 20. There are also ceramics, medieval weapons, Renaissance paintings and sculptures.

✚ J7 ✉ Piazza de' Mozzi 1 ☎ 055 234 2427 🕐 Closed for restoration at time of publication 🚌 B, C ♿ Good 💲 Moderate

MUSEO MARINO MARINI

One of Florence's oldest churches (9th century, with a 15th-century façade and porch) is now a museum dedicated to the sculptor Marino Marini (1901–80), who studied in Florence. An excellent reminder that Italian art didn't grind to a halt in the 17th century.

✚ aIII ✉ Piazza San Pancrazio (Via della Spada) ☎ 055 219 432 🕐 Mon, Wed–Sat 10–5; Sun 10–1. Occasional late opening in Jun/Jul. Closed Aug 🚌 6, 11, 36, 37 ♿ Good 💲 Moderate

'LA SPECOLA': MUSEO ZOOLOGICO

La Specola is so called after the observatory that used to be here. Highlights are the *Cere Anatomiche*, a gruesome set of 18th-century wax models of bits of human bodies. Four vignettes of the plague in Florence show rats eating the intestines of decaying bodies.

✚ H7 ✉ Via Romana 17 ☎ 055 222 451 🕐 Thu–Tue 9–1 🚌 11, 36, 37 ♿ Few 💲 Moderate

Museo Archeologico

MUSEO DI 'FIRENZE COM'ERA'

Paintings and maps showing how Florence used to look from the late 15th until the early 20th centuries. You'll also find delightful 16th-century lunettes of the Medici villas, and the *Pianta della Catena*, an 1887 copy of a 1470 view of Florence.

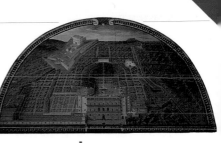

🕂 bIII ✉ Via dell'Oriuolo 24 ☎ 055 239 8483 🕐 Fri–Wed 9–2 🚍 14, 23, B 🔈 Acceptable 🎟 Inexpensive

MUSEO FRATELLI ALINARI

A collection of black-and-white photographs of the Fratelli Alinari company, which was founded in 1852. Temporary photographic exhibitions are also held. It is housed in the 15th-century Palazzo Rucellai.

🕂 aIII ✉ Via della Vigna Nuova 16 ☎ 055 213 370 🕐 Mon, Tue, Thu, Sun 10–7:30; Fri, Sat 10AM–11:30PM (late openings are subject to change) 🚍 6, 11, 36, 37 🔈 Good 🎟 Moderate

MUSEO NAZIONALE DI ANTROPOLOGIA E L'ETNOGRAFIA

Founded in 1869, this museum offers something more than art and history. Exhibits relating to the Kafiri people of Pakistan are academically interesting; the peoples of the areas of Africa that came under Italian colonial rule are well represented.

🕂 bIII ✉ Palazzo Nonfinito, Via del Proconsolo 12 ☎ 055 239 6449 🕐 Wed–Mon 9–1 🚍 14, 23 🔈 Good 🎟 Moderate

MUSEO STIBBERT

A quirky museum of 50,000 pieces gathered by the Italian-Scottish eccentric Frederick Stibbert. It has one of the world's finest collections of armour, and all manner of curiosities, including Stibbert's dress kilt.

🕂 H4 ✉ Via Federico Stibbert 26 ☎ 055 486 049 🕐 Apr–Oct: Mon–Wed 10–1; Fri–Sun 10–6. Nov–Mar: Mon–Wed 10–2; Fri–Sun 10–6 🚍 31, 32 🎟 Moderate ❓ Guided tours only (on the hour) except Sun when visitors are free to wander

OPIFICIO E MUSEO DELLE PIETRE DURE

This small museum is a workshop showing the techniques of working semi-precious stones.

🕂 bII ✉ Via degli Alfani 78 ☎ 055 294 145 🕐 Mon, Wed–Sat 8:15–2; Tue 8:15–7 (subject to change) 🚍 6, 31, 32 🔈 Good 🎟 Inexpensive

SALVATORE FERRAGAMO SHOE MUSEUM

Founded in 1995, this collection of 10,000 pairs of shoes by Ferragamo dates from his return from Hollywood to Florence in 1927 until his death in the 1960s.

🕂 aIV ✉ Palazzo Spini Feroni, Via de' Tornabuoni 14 ☎ 055 336 0456 🕐 Visits by appointment only 🚍 6, 11, 31, 32, 36, 37 🔈 Good 🎟 Free

Museo di 'Firenze com'era'

ART EXHIBITIONS

A number of galleries in addition to the museums listed here have changing exhibitions. These include the Spedale degli Innocenti (➤ 47), the Palazzo Medici-Riccardi (➤ 34) and Casa Buonarroti (➤ 56).

19TH-CENTURY COLLECTORS' MUSEUMS

Florence has three museums that evolved out of somewhat eccentric private collections of the 19th century – the Museo Stibbert, the Museo Bardini and the better known but less interesting Museo Horne:

🕂 J7 ✉ Via dei Benci 6 ☎ 055 244 661 🕐 Mon–Sat 9–1. Closed hols 🚍 B, C 🔈 None 🎟 Moderate 🚊 Santa Croce (➤ 49)

Exhibits in the Museo Bardini

53

Churches

PASSPORT TO HEAVEN?

For centuries the focus of Florence's life, churches contain some of the city's best art. In the Middle Ages, many of Florence's bankers attempted to assuage their guilt for being so rich by paying for a chapel to be decorated with frescos of uplifting spiritual themes (often featuring the patrons). The chapels are invariably named after them – the Bardi Chapel in Santa Croce, for example, and the Strozzi and Tornabuoni chapels in Santa Maria Novella.

BADIA FIORENTINA

The Badia Fiorentina, the oldest monastery in Florence, was founded in AD 978 by Willa, widow of Umberto, Margrave of Tuscany. It is best known in connection with Dante, who used to meet Beatrice here. Its magnificent bell tower, which is Romanesque at the base and Gothic at the top, is one of the most characteristic features of the Florentine skyline. Inside are two fine works of art, namely Filippino Lippi's *The Madonna Appearing to St Bernard*, to the left of the entrance, and the tomb of Count Ugo, son of Willa and Umberto, which is nearby. The two-storey *Chiostro degli Aranci* (orange tree cloister) has charming frescos of the life of St Bernard, by an unknown artist (*c*1440).

➕ bIII ✉ Via del Proconsolo/Piazza San Firenze ☎ 055 287 389 ⏰ Thu–Tue 5AM–7PM; Sun 7:30–11:30 (subject to change) ▣ In the pedestrian zone ♿ Poor 🎟 Free

Fresco from the Badia Fiorentina

OGNISSANTI

This was the parish church of the Vespucci family, one of whose members, Amerigo, named the continent of America after himself. In the second chapel on the right facing the altar is a fresco by Ghirlandaio which is said to include Amerigo's portrait (the boy standing behind the Virgin, with a man in a red cloak to his right). It was also the church of Botticelli's family, and he was buried here. In the *cenacolo* (refectory) there are more Ghirlandaio pieces – a *Last Supper* and *St Jerome in his Study* – and Botticelli's *St Augustine in his Study*.

➕ H6 ✉ Borgo Ognissanti 42 ☎ 055 239 6802 ⏰ Daily 8–noon, 4–6:30 ▣ At the station ♿ Acceptable 🎟 Free

SANTA MARIA MADDALENA DEI PAZZI

Although the original church dates from the 13th century, most of the present building is a

Renaissance rebuild designed by Guiliano da Sangallo at the end of the 15th century. The spectacular interior decoration, with its coloured marble and trompe l'oeil, dates from the baroque. The highlight here, however, is in the chapter house (reached via the crypt) where there is a fresco of the Crucifixion and saints done by Perugino in the 1490s. The lovingly detailed background of a Tuscan landscape is typical of his works.

✚ cIII ☒ Borgo Pinti ◷ Daily 9–noon, 5–7 🚌 6 ♿ Poor 🎟 Inexpensive

Ghirlandaio's Miracle of the Boy brought back to Life *in Santa Trinita*

SANTA FELICITÀ

This is the second oldest church in Florence, dating to the 2nd century AD, when Syrian and Greek merchants settled here. The highlight is the Mannerist *Deposition* (1525–8) by Pontormo, in the Cappella Caponi, immediately on your right as you enter. It is a stunning vortex of improbable forms and colours: lime green, bubblegum pink, acid yellow. On the wall is a charming *Annunciation*, also by Pontormo.

✚ aIV ☒ Piazza Santa Felicita ☎ 055 213 018 ◷ Daily 8–noon, 3:30–6:30 🚌 B, C ♿ Poor 🎟 Free

SANTA TRINITA

The baroque façade of Santa Trinita gives no indication of its austere and tranquil interior. The church dates from 1092 and was rebuilt between 1258 and 1280 in a sparse version of the Gothic. To the far right of the high altar as you face it, the Sassetti Chapel is decorated with frescos showing scenes from the life of St Francis by Ghirlandaio (1483) and including portraits of Francesco Sassetti, the patron of the chapel, and his wife, who are shown on either side of the altar.

✚ aIII ☒ Piazza Santa Trinita ☎ 055 216 912 ◷ Mon–Sat 8–12, 4–6; Sun 4–6 🚌 6, 11, 31, 32, 36, 37 ♿ Good 🎟 Free

SANTO SPIRITO

Designed by Filippo Brunelleschi in 1435, this church acquired a baroque façade in the 18th century. The interior is gloomy, but Filippino Lippi's excellent *Madonna and Child* (1466) is in the Nerli Chapel in the south transept. The *cenacolo* (refectory) houses 11th-century sculpture and a beautiful Gothic *Crucifixion*, believed to be by the followers of Andrea Orcagna.

✚ aIV ☒ Piazza Santo Spirito ☎ 055 210 030 ◷ Thu–Tue 8–12, 4–6; Wed 8–12 🚌 C, 6 ♿ Poor 🎟 Free **Refectory** ☎ 055 287 043 ◷ Tue–Sun 10–1. Closed hols ♿ Good 🎟 Moderate

SANTO STEFANO AL PONTE

This little church, which dates from AD 969, is tucked into a courtyard just behind the Ponte Vecchio. The exterior is a Romanesque delight, added in the 1230s.

✚ bIV ☒ Piazza Santo Stefano al Ponte ◷ Closed for restoration 🚌 In the pedestrian zone

DRESS CODE

Florence's churches may contain some of the most important works of art in the world but try not forget that they are also (and indeed, primarily) places of worship and spiritual, rather than purely artistic, contemplation. All visitors are expected to be appropriately dressed; shoulders and upper arms should be covered and shorts or very short skirts aren't welcome. Try to avoid visiting during services or disturbing those who come in to pray.

An altarpiece within Santo Spirito

Michelangelo in Florence

LIFE OF GENIUS

Michelangelo Buonarroti (1475–1564) was born in Caprese, about 97km east of Florence, but his family came to the city very soon after his birth. When he began his apprenticeship at the age of 13, his teacher, Ghirlandaio, was astounded by his skill, and within a year Michelangelo had left his studies. Initially his patron was Lorenzo the Magnificent but with the political turbulence of the times he was exiled in 1494. He returned to Florence in 1501 and sculpted *David*. He next returned from Rome to Florence in 1516 to sculpt the Medici tombs in San Lorenzo. In 1534 he left Florence for good; he died in Rome but is buried in Santa Croce in Florence. Although Michelangelo painted, made frescos, designed buildings and wrote poetry, he regarded himself primarily as a sculptor.

CASA BUONARROTI

This house, which Michelangelo bought in 1508, is now a fascinating museum and gallery. Exhibits include the artist's earliest known work, the *Madonna della Scala* (*c*1491), a wood and wax model (the only one of its type) of a river god and a model of the façade for San Lorenzo that was never executed.
➕ cIII ✉ Via Ghibellina 70 ☎ 055 241 752 🚇 14 🕐 Wed–Mon 9:30–2 ♿ Good 🎫 Expensive

BARGELLO SCULPTURES

The Bargello (➤ 44) houses three sculptures by Michelangelo: *Bacchus Drunk* (1497), his earliest freestanding work; *Brutus* (1539–40), his only bust, sculpted after the murder of Duke Alessandro de' Medici as a statement against tyranny; and the tondo of the *Madonna and Child with the infant St John* (1503–5), a fine example of his low relief style.
➕ bIII ✉ Via del Proconsolo 4 ☎ 055 238 8606 🕐 Daily 8:15–1:50. Closed 1st, 3rd, 5th Sun and 2nd, 4th Mon of month 🚇 19 ♿ Good 🎫 Moderate

THE *DONI TONDO* IN THE UFFIZI

The *Doni Tondo* (1504–5), the only easel painting that Michelangelo came near to finishing, breaks new ground by showing the infant Jesus above Mary's shoulder, rather than in her lap. The figures' contorted postures were much copied by Mannerists.
➕ bIV ✉ Loggiato degli Uffizi 6 ☎ 055 238 8651 🕐 Tue–Sun 8:15–6:50. Closed 1 May ♿ Good 🎫 Expensive

THE *VICTORY*, PALAZZO VECCHIO

Michelangelo began painting frescos for the Sala dei Cinquecento in the Palazzo Vecchio, but these came to nothing. There is a sculpture by Michelangelo: the *Victory*, opposite the entrance of the Sala dei Cinquecento, which shows a young man holding down the figure of adversity.
➕ bIV ✉ Piazza della Signoria ☎ 055 276 8465 🕐 Mon–Wed, Fri, Sat 9–7; Thu, Sun 9–2. Late opening in summer Mon, Fri. Closed Easter Sun, 1 May, 15 Aug 🚇 19, 23, 31, 32 ♿ Good 🎫 Expensive

One of the Prisoners *now in the Accademia*

Views

FORTE DI BELVEDERE

This fortress was built by the Medici in 1590, ostensibly to protect Florence from attackers, but actually as a refuge for the Medici Grand Dukes in their struggle against the Florentine Republic and as a reminder of Medici military might. There are fabulous views and this is a lovely place to come and sunbathe or have a picnic. In the middle of the fortress there is a three-storey *palazzetto* in the manner of a Medici villa, used to house exhibitions. For these an entrance fee is charged, otherwise the fortress is free.

✚ H7 ✉ Costa di San Giorgio and Via di Belvedere 🕐 Daily 9–6 (later in summer and when there is an exhibition) 🚍 No bus ♿ Impossible 💲 Free

MUSEO DI ORSANMICHELE

Behind Orsanmichele on the Via dell'Arte di Lana is the Palazzo dell'Arte di Lana, which is the entrance for the Museum of Orsanmichele, actually the two upper storeys of the church. Climb up for fantastic views of the rooftops of central Florence.

✚ aIII ✉ Palazzo dell'Arte di Lana, Via dell'Arte di Lana 🕐 Closed for restoration at time of publication 🚍 In the pedestrian zone ♿ Impossible 💲 Free

PIAZZALE MICHELANGELO

Despite the fact that Piazzale Michelangelo is frequented by bus loads of tourists, this stupendous vantage point is still very much worth the trip, either by bus or by foot. Ignore the poor green copy of Michelangelo's *David* and the rapidly mushrooming crop of souvenir stalls, beware of pickpockets and soak up the wonderful view.

✚ J7 ✉ Piazzale Michelangelo, off Viale Galileo Galilei 🚍 12, 13 ♿ Good 💲 Free

PONTE SANTA TRINITA

One of the best places to view the Ponte Vecchio.

✚ aIV ✉ Ponte Santa Trinita 🚍 6, 11, 36, 37, C ♿ Good 💲 Free

HILLTOP VISTAS

E M Forster put the idea of a 'room with a view' in Florence on the map. There are wonderful views from hotel rooms across terracotta roofs, but perhaps the most breathtaking vistas are from the hills that surround the city, both close up – for example from the Forte di Belvedere, integrated into the medieval walls – and from a distance, typically from Fiesole (▶ 20), where people go to see the lights by night.

Looking across the rooftops to the Bargello

57

Parks, Gardens & Open Spaces

RARE COMMODITY

Given the Renaissance artists' veneration for nature, it is ironic that Florence is so bereft of greenery. So make the most of such green spaces as there are, including Forte di Belvedere (➤ 57) and the Villa Medicea di Poggio a Caiano, with its English-style gardens.

LE CASCINE

Florence's largest park is a long way from the town centre, and is tacky (badly kept and given to seediness at night) when you eventually get there. Long (3km) and thin (sometimes as narrow as 100m), it was laid out as a public park by Napoleon's sister Elisa Baciocchi Bonaparte in 1811, on the site of the Medici dairy pastures (*cascine*). There is a lively market on Tuesday and one of Florence's open-air swimming pools is also in the park.

➕ G6 ✉ Ponte della Vittoria 🚌 17c ♿ Good 🎫 Free

GARDEN TOURS

From May to October you can visit some of Florence's grandest villas and their gardens, not normally open to the public because they are privately owned. Contact the tourist office for details.

☎ 055 288 049

GIARDINO DEI SEMPLICI

This oasis of neat greenery, the botanical garden of Florence University, is on the site of a garden laid out in 1545–46 for Cosimo I, who wanted to keep up with the Pisans and Genoans. It is named after the medicinal plants (*semplici*) grown here in addition to water plants, Tuscan flora, irises and shrubs. There are also greenhouses with tropical palms, ferns, orchids and citrus fruits.

➕ cII ✉ Via Micheli 3 🕐 Mon–Sat 9–1 🚌 10, 11, 17, 20 ♿ Good 🎫 Free

Giardino dei Semplici

PIAZZA DELLA REPUBBLICA

This grandiose square in the middle of Florence, on the site of the old market, was built in the 1870s, when Florence briefly was the capital of Italy. Florentines are not fond of the square's architecture nor its crass neoclassical triumphal arch, but it is an unusually large open space, where you can breathe a little and let a child run free. All around are grand cafés, and in the centre old men gather to discuss the day's affairs.

➕ bIII ♿ Good

What's Free

In the Top 25

STROLLING THE STREETS

Half the appeal of Florence is the fact that it is eminently walkable – just to wander its streets and bridges is enormously pleasurable. Much of the best art in Florence is to be found in churches (▶ 54–55), where, in most instances, there is no entrance charge.

MUSEUMS WITHOUT ENTRANCE FEES

The Florentine aptitude for making money is alive and thriving now just as it was in the time of the Medici. In short, there is not a great deal to be had for free in Florence! However, exceptions include the city's many views, its churches and Salvatore Ferragamo Shoe Museum (▶ 53).

PARKS WITHOUT ENTRANCE FEES

The Giardino di Boboli entry fee, imposed in 1992, was extremely unpopular with Florentines, who had relied upon it for fresh air and greenery. Now, all that remain free are the small Giardino dei Semplici and the less-than-lovely Cascine.
Giardino dei Semplici 🔲 cII ✉ Via Micheli 3 🕐 Mon, Fri 9–noon, 2:30–5; Wed 2:30–5 🚌 10, 11, 17
Cascine 🔲 G6 ✉ Ponte della Vittoria 🚌 17c

WALKS AND VIEWS

Take a walk along the medieval city walls, passing through the Forte di Belvedere and Piazzale Michelangelo (▶ 24, 57).

TICKET TO RIDE

When you have had enough of walking you can take a wonderful tour of suburban Florence for the price of a single bus ticket. The No. 12 and No.

Crossing the Arno

13 buses do a loop around Florence (clockwise and anti-clockwise respectively) that lasts about one hour, starting and finishing at the train station. You do grind through some of the less picturesque suburbs, but the buses also wind along the leafy boulevards, such as Viale Machiavelli in the hills south of Florence, where you can ogle the fabulous villas of the rich and famous. If you want to go a little farther out into the countryside take bus No. 7 to Fiesole (🔲 M2) or No. 13 to the pretty little town of Settignano east of Florence. Both buses leave from the train station.

For Children

Il Porcellino, *in the Mercato Nuovo*

ARMOUR

For the child into medieval knights, a trip to the Museo Stibbert (➤ 53), which has one of the best collections of armour in the world, would be the highlight of Florence. The Bargello (➤ 44) also has a fine collection of arms and armour.

CLIMBS, WALKS, VIEWS AND PARKS

The physical exertion and visual exhilaration of climbing towers and walking along city walls can be appealing. You can climb both the bell tower and the dome of the cathedral. The walk to San Miniato (➤ 50) encompasses a stretch of the medieval city walls as well as the fortress of the Belvedere, which is fascinating for a child with an interest in castles and military architecture. If yours simply need to blow off steam, head for the Boboli Gardens (➤ 29) or Le Cascine (➤ 58).

MICHELANGELO'S *DAVID*

The story of David is one that some children know and many will identify with. Michelangelo's sculpture *David* has a very immediate physical impact. Furthermore, you can encourage your children to compare the original in the Galleria dell'Accademia (➤ 45) with the copies – one outside the Palazzo Vecchio (➤ 43) and one (much reviled) on the Piazzale Michelangelo (➤ 57).

SAN MARCO

The monks' cells in San Marco, each with a painting by Fra Angelico, provide a rare instance of art in its original context, and the cells evoke the monks' life in a way that can capture a child's imagination. Fra Angelico's *Annunciation* expresses a moment in the story of the Nativity that many children will know.

SHOPPING AND CLOTHES

Football shirts, a big hit with both boys and girls, can be found in sports shops such as Diadora (➤ 74) and much cheaper in the Mercato San Lorenzo (➤ 75). The markets also have cheap leather and sheepskin gloves and slippers, and the Mercato Nuovo has the brass boar, *Il Porcellino* (➤ 62). If your children are fashion mad, try the Salvatore Ferragamo Shoe Museum (➤ 53, 72) and the Museum of Costume in the Palazzo Pitti (➤ 28).

SPORT

If Fiorentina are playing football, a trip to the stadium is a real wow (➤ 84). Or try the swimming pool at Le Cascine (➤ 58) or go canoeing along the River Arno (➤ 84).

The River Arno & its Bridges

THE RIVER ARNO
The River Arno has been crucial to the history of Florence, providing water for the textile industry on which the city's prosperity was based.

PONTE ALLA CARRAIA
The city's second oldest bridge was built around 1218 and reconstructed after floods in 1269 and 1333; the current bridge was rebuilt after World War II as a copy of the 16th-century bridge. The name comes from the carts (*carri*) that carried cloth between the cloth-making districts of San Freddiano on the south side and Ognissanti on the north side of the bridge.
✚ aIV

PONTE ALLE GRAZIE
First constructed in 1237, when it was known as Ponte Rubaconte (the bridge over the River Rubicon), it was rebuilt after World War II to a modern design. It takes its name from the oratory of Santa Maria delle Grazie, which once stood here.
✚ bIV

THE LUNGARNI
Along the roads that hug the banks of the Arno – the *Lungarni* – you'll find some of the finest palaces in Florence: the baroque Palazzo Corsini on Lungarno Corsini, with its private art collection, and the Palazzo Spini-Ferroni on Lungarno degli Accaiuoli, which houses the Salvatore Ferragamo Shoe Emporium (► 72).
✚ aIV–bIV

PONTE SANTA TRINITA
The finest of Florence's bridges dates as far back as 1252, although what you see today is a very well-executed replica of Ammannati's bridge built in 1567 and destroyed by the Nazis in 1944. Ammannati was commissioned by Cosimo I and probably consulted Michelangelo in his designs. Some of the loveliest views of Florence, especially the Ponte Vecchio, are to be had from here.
✚ aIV ✉ Ponte Santa Trinita 🚌 6, 11, 31, 32, 36, 37
♿ Good 🎟 Free

FLOOD FACTS
In November 1966 the River Arno burst its banks to disastrous effect: the tide marks noted all over the city bear witness to the immense weight of water and sludge that bludgeoned through the streets, reaching as high as 6m in the Santa Croce region. This was not the only flood there has ever been, however: bridges were swept away in 1269 and 1333, and the city was submerged in 1557 and 1884, but not as badly as in 1966.

Sunset over the Arno

Markets

Surveying the range of goods for sale in the Mercato Nuovo

TO MARKET, TO MARKET

Florence markets give you the opportunity to participate in everyday Florentine life. Planning a daily picnic lunch is an excellent excuse to go shopping.

MERCATO DELLE CASCINE

Florence's biggest general market, selling everything from fresh food to household and cooking equipment, is held every Tuesday in Le Cascine (➤ 58, 75).

✚ G6　☒ Viale Abramo Lincoln　🚌 1, 9, 12

MERCATO CENTRALE

The largest of Florence's produce markets is held in the magnificent cast-iron structure of the Mercato Centrale, built in 1874, with an extra floor added in 1980. Just about every kind of fresh food is sold here.

✚ all　☒ Piazza Mercato Centrale　🕐 Mon–Fri 7–2; Sat 7–2, 4–7:30　🍴 Yes　🚌 10, 12, 25, 31, 32　♿ Good (but crowded)

MERCATO DELLE PULCI

The Piazza dei Ciompi, traditionally the heart of the working-class area of Florence, is a fitting spot for the flea market. The goods generally come under the heading of 'junk' but prices cannot be said to match.

✚ cIII　☒ Piazza dei Ciompi　🚌 B　♿ Good

MERCATO DI SANT'AMBROGIO

After the Mercato Centrale, this is the second most important market for fresh produce in Florence. It is favoured by Florence's working population and is very cheap as well as pleasantly noisy.

✚ dIII　☒ Piazza Sant'Ambrogio　🕐 Mon–Fri 7–2　🍴 Yes　🚌 B　♿ Good

MERCATO NUOVO

So called to distinguish it from the Mercato Vecchio, which used to be on the site of what is now the Piazza della Repubblica, this market is most famous for the engaging brass boar with a shiny, well-stroked nose, *Il Porcellino*, which sometimes lends its name to the market. It is also known as the 'straw market', a reference to the straw hats historically sold here, and still to be found.

✚ bIII　☒ Piazza Mercato Nuovo　🕐 Summer: Mon–Sat. Winter: Tue–Sun　🍴 Yes　🚌 In the pedestrian zone　♿ Good (but crowded)

MERCATO SAN LORENZO

The Mercato San Lorenzo is fun, touristy and very centrally located, in the shadow of the church of San Lorenzo. There are lots of stalls selling leather goods, many of which are genuinely good value, but go armed with a healthy scepticism (➤ 72). In the souvenir category you will find T-shirts with lewd designs and artistic clichés, aprons, football shirts and paper goods (➤ 78) including delightful calendars.

✚ bIII　☒ Piazza San Lorenzo　🕐 Summer: Mon–Sat 8–7. Winter: Tue–Sun 8–7　🍴 Yes　🚌 In the pedestrian zone　♿ Good

FLORENCE
where to...

Elegant Restaurants

PRICES

Expect to pay per person for a meal, excluding drink

£   up to 13 euros/L25,000
££   up to 26 euros/L50,000
£££   over 26 euros/L50,000

Until recently almost all Italian restaurants added a cover charge (*coperto*), usually 1–2.50 euros/L2,000–L5,000. This was said to cover the bread and the table linen and was separate from the service charge (*servizio*), which is about 10 per cent. However, the authorities are now trying to discourage this charge.

RESTAURANT ETIQUETTE

Italians have a strongly developed sense of how to behave, which applies in restaurants as much as anywhere else. It is bad form to order only one course in any restaurant (if that is what you want, go to a *pizzeria*). And the concept of a doggy bag could not be more at odds with Italian ideas of eating out. You might succeed in getting one if you want, but you will pay a very high price in the loss of your dignity. Italians do not get drunk in public; to do so is to make a *brutissima figura*, an appalling impression.

ALLE MURATE (£££)

This is one of those places where traditional Tuscan favourites are given a twist. You can choose from one of two menus – the Tuscan and the innovative. There's also a good range of fish, game and offal-based dishes.

➕ dIV ✉ Via Ghibellina 52r ☎ 055 240 618 🕐 Closed lunch and Mon 🚌 6, 14

CANTINETTA ANTINORI (££)

A refined setting for the chic Florentine elite. The food comes from the farm of the Antinori family, whose wines are world renowned. Dress up or you are likely to feel completely out of place.

➕ alII ✉ Piazza Antinori 3 ☎ 055 292 234 🕐 Closed Sat, Sun 🚌 6, 11, 31, 37

CARPE DIEM (££)

It's worth making the trek out to Fiesole at lunch or dinner for the fine, innovative dishes that are served on a spectacular summer terrace with views over the city.

➕ M3 ✉ Via Giuseppe Mantellini 2b, Fiesole ☎ 055 599 595 🕐 Closed Mon 🚌 Bus to Fiesole from station

IL CIBREO (££)

This restaurant near the market of Sant'Ambrogio offers no pasta but instead an intriguing range of robust Florentine dishes, some made with less familiar parts of the animal such as tripe and cockscombs. In all cases the food is first class. There is also an inexpensive section (➤ 66).

➕ dIII ✉ Via dei Macci 118r ☎ 055 234 1100 🕐 Closed Sun, Mon 🚌 14, B

DINO (££)

The unprepossessing exterior hides a cool, airy dining area, with beautifully vaulted ceilings and sparse decoration. A range of sophisticated but unfussy food is prepared in the open kitchen. The wine cellar is exceptionally good. During peak season there are sometimes groups in the early evenings; arrive after 8PM to avoid them.

➕ dIV ✉ Via Ghibellina 51r ☎ 055 241 452 🕐 Closed Sun evening, Mon 🚌 14

ENOTECA PINCHIORRI (£££)

The city's most fashionable and priciest eatery is somewhat serious. For wine connoisseurs it is a must, possessing one of Europe's very finest wine cellars. The *menù degustazione* includes wines appropriate to each course.

➕ cIV ✉ Via Ghibellina 87 ☎ 055 242 777 🕐 Closed Sun, Mon and Wed lunch 🚌 14

SABATINI (£££)

One of Italy's best tables, Sabatini is still chic, if no longer quite what it once was. However, it remains both extremely good and pleasantly old-fashioned.

➕ alII ✉ Via dei Panzani 9a ☎ 055 211 559 🕐 Closed Mon 🚌 6, 9, 11

Tuscan & Florentine Cuisine

ANTICA TRATTORIA ORESTE (££)
A delightful trattoria with outdoor seating, a menu of robust main courses and pasta dishes such as penne with lemon and arugula.
➕ alV ✉ Piazza Santo Spirito 16r ☎ 055 238 2383 🕐 Closed Tue 🚇 B

BALDINI (££)
Garibaldi ate here, and it's a popular Florentine lunch spot between Santa Maria Novella and the park of Le Cascine. Try the homemade gnocchi (potato dumplings) with tomatoes and mushrooms.
➕ G6 ✉ Via Il Prato 96r ☎ 055 287 663 🕐 Closed Sat and Sun evening 🚇 1, 9, 12, 26, 27, 35

LA BARAONDA (££)
Baraonda means chaos but there is nothing chaotic about the carefully prepared traditional dishes served in this bustling, informal place. Popular with the locals.
➕ dlV ✉ Via Ghibellina 67r ☎ 055 234 1171 🕐 Closed Sun, Mon, lunch in winter 🚇 14

IL CINGHIALE BIANCO (££)
The White Boar is named after one of Tuscany's greatest culinary specialities.
➕ alV ✉ Borgo San Jacopo 43 ☎ 055 215 706 🕐 Closed Tue and Wed 🚇 3, 13, 32

COCO LEZZONE (£££)
A Florentine favourite with informal white-tiled rooms. The short menu offers Tuscan classics.
➕ alll ✉ Via del Parioncino 26r ☎ 055 287 178 🕐 Closed Sun and Tue evening 🚇 C

GARGA (££)
A lively, arty bistro with a fashionable clientele.
➕ alll ✉ Via del Moro 48r ☎ 055 239 8898 🕐 Closed Mon 🚇 6, 11

IL LATINI (£)
Boisterous restaurant offering Tuscan classics such as *pappardelle con la lepre* (wide strips of pasta with hare sauce). Seating is at communal tables.
➕ alll ✉ Via Palchetti 6r ☎ 055 210 916 🕐 Closed Mon 🚇 6, 11

OSTERIA DE' BENCI (£)
A genuine Florentine *osteria*. Start with *crostini* (Tuscan *bruschetta* – toasted bread served with spreads, cheeses and cold meats) then choose from the day's menu that often includes spaghetti in red wine and/or a delicious vegetable soup. The meat is particularly good.
➕ clV ✉ Via de' Benci ☎ 055 234 4923 🕐 Closed Sun and Aug 🚇 14

PONTE VECCHIO (££)
Good eatery specialising in mushroom dishes. Popular with tourists.
➕ blV ✉ Lungarno Archibusieri 8r ☎ 055 292 289 🕐 Closed Mon 🚇 In the pedestrian zone

QUATTRO LEONI (££)
An attractive place with outdoor seating and excellent food.
➕ alV ✉ Via Vellutini 1r ☎ 055 218 562 🕐 Closed Sun 🚇 11, 36, 37, 68

NATURALLY ROBUST
The classic Florentine dish is *bistecca alla fiorentina* (T-bone steak sold by the weight, usually 100g). Grilled and served rare with lemon, it can be found in the majority of Florentine restaurants.

Other specialities include *trippa alla fiorentina* (tripe stewed with tomatoes and served with parmesan), *crostini* (toasted bread and a pâté of roughly chopped chicken livers), *panzanella* (a salad of crumbled bread tossed with tomatoes with olive oil, onions, basil and parsley) and *pappa con pomodoro* (a thick cold soup of bread and tomatoes). The classic Tuscan dessert is *biscotti di Prato* – hard and dry almond biscuits dunked in *vin santo* (fortified wine). *Zucotto* is a dome-shaped confection of alcohol-soaked madeira cake, whipped cream, nuts and chopped chocolate.

Budget, Ethnic & Vegetarian Fare

SOMETHING ITALIAN

In Italy you will probably find the same dishes in a budget trattoria as in the most expensive restaurants. The difference is primarily one of ambience and decor and – frequently – the wine list.

BREAD

Almost all bread in Tuscany is made without salt. This takes some getting used to, but the blandness makes a good background to highly flavoured foods such as Florentine salami *Finocchiona*, which is scented with fennel and garlic. And the bread's texture – firm, almost coarse, and very substantial – is wonderful. Strict laws govern what goes into Italian bread: it is free of chemical preservatives.

ACQUACOTTA (£)

A reliable trattoria named after a Tuscan soup (literally 'cooked water'). The menu covers other dishes, however, including *bollito*, mixed boiled meats with herb sauce.
🚌 cIII ✉ Via dei Pilastri 51r
☎ 055 242 907 🕐 Closed Tue evening, Wed, Aug 🚌 B

AMON (£)

An Egyptian snack bar, not far from the station, serving bread filled with tasty delicacies, including falafel.
🚌 aIII ✉ Via Palazzuolo 26–28r ☎ 055 293 146
🕐 Closed Sun 🚌 36, 37

BELLE DONNE (£)

A cheap option in an expensive part of town. It's small, modest and you can barely see inside because of the cascades of potted plants. The menu has some interestingly prepared vegetables.
🚌 aIII ✉ Via delle Belle Donne 16r ☎ 055 238 2609
🕐 Closed Sat evening and Sun 🚌 6, 9, 11

BENVENUTO (£)

This basic, inexpensive traditional trattoria lies between Piazza della Signoria and Santa Croce. It serves Tuscan staples and is popular with visitors and locals alike.
🚌 bIV ✉ Via della Mosca 15r, corner of Via dei Neri ☎ 055 214 833 🕐 Closed Wed and Sun 🚌 6, 14

IL CARMINE (£)

Small, friendly trattoria in the delightful Piazza del Carmine. Lengthy (difficult) menu of traditional dishes.
🚌 H7 ✉ Piazza del Carmine 18r ☎ 055 218 601
🕐 Closed Sun 🚌 B

LA CASALINGA (£)

This busy family-run establishment is a good place to try *ribollita*, the thick Florentine soup made with bread and vegetables.
🚌 aIV ✉ Via dei Michelozzi 9r
🕐 Closed Sun 🚌 6, 11, 31, 32, 36, 37

IL CIBREO (£–££)

At the back of this mid-range restaurant you can eat the same food for a fraction of the price – but you won't be encouraged (or indeed, welcome) to loiter. A steal.
🚌 dIII ✉ Via dei Macci 118
☎ 055 234 1100 🕐 Closed Sun and Mon 🚌 14

DA SERGIO (£)

A basic but very good trattoria with a different menu every day. Hidden behind the Mercato San Lorenzo, it is not the easiest place to find and it's open only for lunch, but it's worth a detour.
🚌 bII ✉ Piazza San Lorenzo 8r ☎ 055 281 941 🕐 Closed evenings, Sun and Aug 🚌 In the pedestrian zone

FUORIPORTA (££)

The wine bar of the moment is near San Miniato al Monte. In the evening, cheeses, cold meats and *crostini* are served; at lunchtime, pasta dishes and desserts. The wine list is vast (more than 600) and there are also whiskies and *eaux de vie* for serious tasters.

✚ J8 ✉ Via Monte alle Croci 10r ☎ 055 234 2483
🕐 Closed Mon 🚌 12, 13, 38

IL MANDARINO (££–£££)

A centrally located Chinese restaurant.

✚ bIII ✉ Via della Condotta 17r ☎ 055 239 6130
🕐 Closed Mon 🚶 In the pedestrian zone

LE MOSSACCE (£–££)

Bustling eatery between the Duomo and the Bargello; excellent Tuscan food including rich soups.

✚ bIII ✉ Via del Proconsolo 55r ☎ 055 294 361
🕐 Closed Sat, Sun, Mon evenings and Aug 🚌 14, 23

MISTER HANG (££–£££)

This popular Chinese restaurant has air-conditioning. Reservations are a good idea.

✚ cIII ✉ Via Ghibellina 134r ☎ 055 234 4810 🕐 Closed Mon 🚌 14

PALLE D'ORO (£)

Spotless and spartan, this restaurant serves good food – which you can take away to eat outside.

✚ aII ✉ Via Sant'Antonino 43r ☎ 055 288 383
🕐 Closed Sun and Aug
🚶 Short walk from the railway station

ROSE'S (£)

Rose's is a modern and sleek bar that serves great cocktails, but is also one of the few places in Florence where you can eat good sushi.

✚ aIII ✉ Via del Parione 26r ☎ 055 287 090 🕐 Closed Sun
🚌 6, 11, 36, 37, A, B

AL TRANVAI (£)

Diners are packed into this lively trattoria in the heart of Florence on the same square as the weekly market. The speciality is *frattaglie* (a mind-boggling range of offal) but the menu changes every day with a range of pastas and soups followed by filling vegetable *contorni*.

✚ G7 ✉ Piazza Torquato Tasso 14 ☎ 055 225 197
🕐 Closed Sat, Sun 🚌 12, 13

TRATTORIA MARIONE (£)

Good home cooking based on simple ingredients. Well-prepared dishes include *bollito* (boiled beef), soups and tripe.

✚ aIII ✉ Via della Spada 27r ☎ 055 214 756 🚶 In the pedestrian zone

RUTH'S (£)

A bright, modern eatery next to the synagogue serving an interesting mix of vegetarian (although fish is also served), Middle Eastern and kosher.

✚ cIII ✉ Via Farini 2a ☎ 055 248 0888 🕐 Closed Fri evening and Sat lunch 🚌 6

ZÀ-ZÀ (£)

An old-fashioned and inexpensive trattoria close to the Mercato Centrale and San Lorenzo market. Good Tuscan food and a fine dining room with dark stone walls lined with old photographs and prints.

✚ bII ✉ Piazza del Mercato Centrale 26r ☎ 055 215 411
🕐 Closed Sun and Aug
🚶 Pedestrian zone

CONTRADICTION

The concept of vegetarianism is not one that sits easily with Italian ideas about food, and there are very few vegetarian restaurants in Italy. However, there are few better countries for those who do not eat meat (or fish). Many pasta dishes contain no meat – pesto, tomato sauce or ravioli stuffed with spinach and ricotta, to name but a few. For a main course, try *grigliata di verdura* (grilled vegetables) or else restaurant stalwarts such as *parmigiana di melanzane* (aubergine layered with tomato and mozzarella, and baked with a parmesan crust), *mozzarella in carrozza* (fried mozzarella) and *fritate* (omelettes). In Tuscany there are also wonderful bean dishes, such as *fagioli all'uccelletto* (white beans with a sage-flavoured tomato sauce). *Pizza margherita* is made with just cheese and tomato (► 68). *Ribollita* is a thick Tuscan soup made with cabbage, beans and other vegetables; to be certain that it is meat-free, be sure to ask.

Pizzas & Snacks

PIZZA AT ITS BEST

As in just about every Italian town, pizzas are all over and many shops sell *pizza a taglio* (cut pizza). One of the best options for a quick snack is a slice. In addition to the standard margherita pizza (tomato and mozzarella), you will find all kinds of other delicious toppings, such as courgette flowers and aubergine. Go when they're busy and the turnover is high to avoid eating cold pizza that's been sitting around for a while. If you do not want a multi-course meal, opt for a pizzeria, where no one will be offended if you have just one course.

BORGO ANTICO (££)

A popular trendy restaurant and pizzeria in the Piazza Santo Spirito. The excellent pizzas as well as the full range of salads, pastas and main courses are served on huge, colourful plates. Book ahead.

✚ aIV ✉ Piazza Santo Spirito 6r ☎ 055 210 437 ⓣ Closed Mon 🚌 B

CANTINETTA DEI VERRAZZANO (££)

An absolutely stunning wine bar-cum-shop selling breads baked on the premises and wines from the Castello di Verrazzano estates near Greve in Chianti Classico. The marble-topped tables are both rustic and sophisticated, like the wines and food. Don't miss the *focaccia* (flat loaf), baked in the wood-burning ovens out back.

✚ bIII ✉ Via dei Tavolini 18–20r ☎ 055 239 8132/268 590 ⓣ Closed Sun 🚌 In the pedestrian zone

LA MESCITA (£)

An unassuming but excellent wine bar in the student area, where hearty wines accompany *crostini* and other delicious snacks.

✚ bII ✉ Via degli Alfani 70r 🚌 6

PROCACCI (£££)

This delightful bar is something of a legend because of its *panini tartufati*, sandwiches made with a white truffle puree. Just the thing with a glass of Tuscan wine at 11AM, as celebrated cookbook author Elizabeth David noted in *Italian Food*.

✚ aIII ✉ Via de' Tornabuoni 64r ☎ 055 211 656 🚌 6, 11, 36, 37

LE SCUDERIE (££)

This bistro in the former *scuderie* (stables) of the convent of Santo Spirito serves pizzas as well as Italian and international fare. Extensive salad bar.

✚ aIV ✉ Via Maffia 31–33r ☎ 055 287 198 ⓣ Closed Mon 🚌 B

LE VOLPI L'UVA (££)

A fabulous wine bar behind the Ponte Vecchio where you can wash down pungent Italian salamis and cheeses with robust Tuscan wines.

✚ aIV ✉ Piazza dei Rossi ☎ 055 239 8132 ⓣ Closed Sun 🚌 B, C

UVAFRAGOLA (£)

Formerly a Chinese restaurant, now a popular pizzeria–trattoria.

✚ aIII ✉ Piazza di Santa Maria Novella 9–10 ☎ 055 215 386 ⓣ Thu–Tue, noon–3, 7–midnight 🚌 Near the railway station

ZANOBINI (£)

A traditional bar where you can drop in for a glass of wine, a slice of salami or cheese and a wedge of rustic bread. Popular with locals.

✚ aII ✉ Via Sant'Antonino 47r ☎ 055 239 6850 ⓣ Mon–Sat 8–2, 3:30–8; closed public hols 🚌 Short walk from the railway station

Ice Cream Parlours

GELATERIA CARABÉ (££)

A top-quality Sicilian ice cream parlour run with tremendous pride by Antonio and Loredana Lisciandro. Gelateria Carabé is the place to have a *granita* in Florence – choose from lemon, coffee, fig, watermelon or even prickly pear. The pistachio *gelato* is outstanding, made with super-flavourful pistachio nuts, grown on the volcanic slopes of Bronte in Sicily, which cost twice as much as other pistachios. Near the Accademia, it's a rare treat not to be missed.

➕ bII ✉ Via Ricasoli 60r ☎ 055 289 476 🚌 In the pedestrian zone

PERCHÉ NO! (££)

'Why not!' has to be a good name for an ice cream parlour. Founded in 1939, this store was such a hit with the GIs when they liberated Florence that they made sure this was the first building in the city to have the electricity reconnected! It is renowned for its *semifreddi*, which come in creamy flavours such as hazelnut mousse and *zuppa inglese* (trifle). The *sorbetti* are also first rate. Particularly favoured by the Florentines, Perché No! is close to Piazza della Signoria.

➕ bIII ✉ Via dei Tavolini 19r ☎ 055 239 8969 🕐 Closed Tue 🚌 In the pedestrian zone

PERSEO (££)

Not exactly off the beaten tourist track but it's excellently placed if you want to get your blood sugar levels up after a hard morning in the Uffizi.

➕ bIII–bIV ✉ Piazza della Signoria 16r ☎ 055 239 8316 🚌 3, 23, 31, 32

VIVOLI (££)

Vivoli is legendary among foreign visitors. It is not so much the range of *gelati* that is exceptional as the quality. Among the more unusual flavours, you will find frozen rice pudding, studded with little nuggets of rice. The fruit flavours include a wonderful green apple, complete with little bits of peel. Close to Piazza Santa Croce, it's a little hard to find – but definitely worth the trouble.

➕ cIII ✉ Via Isola delle Stinche 7r ☎ 055 292 334 🕐 Closed Mon 🚌 Short walk from Piazza Santa Croce, which is served by 23

SHOCKINGLY CLEAR FLAVOURS

Italian ice cream – *gelato* – is generally of very high quality. Italians would rather pay more and eat something made with fresh ingredients. So a basic ice cream is usually made with milk, cream, eggs and sugar, and the flavours are strikingly pure and direct. A favourite flavour is *crema* – egg custard – good with a scoop of intense dark chocolate or pungent coffee. People usually opt for a selection of *creme* or *frutte* (creams or fruit) flavours, and don't mix the two types. Creme include *tiramisù* ('pick-me-up'), *zuppa inglese* (trifle) or a range of chocolates and marrons glacés. The best *gelaterie* serve fruit flavours made from whatever fruits are in season. A few establishments still make their own *granita*, a refreshing shaved ice slush that's sloppier and icier than the fruit *sorbetti* (sorbets), made from just fruit and sugar – no cream or eggs. A *semifreddo* (half cold) is half iced: rather, it's a frozen mousse – softer and lighter in texture than a *gelato*, and less intense in flavour.

Coffee & Pastries

ITALIAN CAKES & COFFEE

There are three main types of Italian cake. *Brioche* (pastries) are made with sweet yeast dough and often filled with a delicious, oozing custard. *Torte* (cakes) tend to be tarts, such as the ubiquitous *torta della nonna* (granny's cake), a kind of cake in tart form, or *torta di ricotta*, in which ricotta is mixed with sugar and candied peel. Then there are all kinds of little cookies, most of which contain nuts and have names such as the accurately named *brutti ma buoni* (ugly but good). Italian coffee, now widely available around the world, is no longer a novelty. Italians start the day with a *brioche* and *cappuccino* – and rarely drink *cappuccino* after about 11AM and never after dinner. *Espresso* is what people have after dinner, or as a quick shot taken standing by the bar; an excuse for a chat (just ask for *caffè*). *Caffè corretto* is 'corrected' with a dash of grappa or other spirit; *caffè macchiato* is 'stained' with milk and *caffè latte* is a milkier version of a *cappuccino*. *Latte macchiato* is hot milk with a dash of coffee.

BAR MAJA (£)

To all appearances this station area bar is unexceptional. However, if you go there in the morning, the barman will happily create delightful *cappuccini* with frothy white milk worked into the shape of a heart or a Florentine lily. The pastries are delicious.
✚ all ✉ Via Luigi Alamanni 9r ☎ 055 218 929 ◷ Closed Sat, Sun ☐ By the railway station

BAR MANARESI (£)

Rumour has it that this is the best cup of coffee in Florence. It's roasted and ground on the premises so you are guaranteed an enticing aroma while you sip.
✚ bIII ✉ Via de Lamberti ◷ Early morning–8PM. Closed Sun ☐ In the pedestrian zone

CENNINI (£)

This has the best *torte della nonna* in Florence.
✚ aIV ✉ Borgo San Jacopo 51r ☎ 055 294 930 ☐ 3, 31, 32

GIACOSA (£££)

An elegant café with a very stylish clientele. Renowned as the place where the Negroni cocktail was invented. Convenient for Gucci.
✚ aIII ✉ Via de' Tornabuoni 83r ☎ 055 239 6226 ◷ Closed Sun ☐ 6, 11, 36, 37

GILLI (£££)

A chic, opulent café in the Piazza della Repubblica; the pastries are renowned (but pricey). Sit outside and indulge in, say, a lavish ice cream sundae.
✚ bIII ✉ Via Roma 1r ☎ 055 239 6310 ◷ Closed Tue ☐ In the pedestrian zone

KAFFEEHAUS (£££)

Go to this café in the Boboli Gardens not so much for the quality of the coffee and pastries as the superb view. The building is a folly dating from 1776.
✚ H7 ✉ In the Boboli Gardens (➤ 29) ◷ 11–dusk ☐ B, C

PASZKOWSKI (£££)

Located on the grandiose Piazza della Repubblica, this is a lovely, if expensive, old-world café and tearoom where a piano bar adds a note of refinement to an already delightful interior.
✚ bIII ✉ Piazza della Repubblica 6r ☎ 055 210 236 ☐ In the pedestrian zone

RIVOIRE (£££)

At Rivoire you pay for the view, but it's worth it. Looking out towards the Palazzo Vecchio, this is the ideal place to relax after a visit to the Uffizi.
✚ bIII ✉ Piazza della Signoria 5r ☎ 055 214 412 ◷ Closed Mon ☐ In the pedestrian zone

ROBIGLIO (££)

The old-fashioned Florentine bar/*pasticceria* par excellence, it opened in 1928. The pastries are to die for.
◷ Mon–Sat 7:30–1:30, 3–8 at: ✚ bIII ✉ Via Tosinghi 11r ☎ 055 215 013 ☐ In the pedestrian zone; ✚ cII ✉ Via dei Servi 112 ☎ 055 214 501 ☐ 12, 14, 23; ✚ bI ✉ Viale S Lavagnini 18r ☎ 055 490 886 ☐ 8

Wine & Food

LA BOLOGNESE
For those who want to take a real bit of Italian cuisine home with them, the fresh pasta made and sold here includes tortellini, ravioli and gnocchi.

✚ H7 ✉ Via dei Serragli 24 ☎ 055 282 318 🚌 6, 11, 36, 37, 68

LA FIASCHETTERIA
A heady aroma of wine pervades this marvellous shop. No frills, just a real sense of pleasure in good wine.

✚ H7 ✉ Via dei Serragli 47r ☎ 055 287 420 🚌 36, 37

MERCATO CENTRALE
The place to observe the care with which Italians buy their food – note the superb fruit and vegetables, meat, poultry, cheeses, breads, salamis and hams.

✚ all ✉ Piazza del Mercato Centrale 🚌 In the pedestrian zone

PAOLO PERI
A no-nonsense wine and oil shop selling quality products in the prestigious Via Maggio.

✚ alV ✉ Via Maggio 5r ☎ 055 212 674 🚌 36, 37

PEGNA
This lovely old-fashioned shop, around since 1860, sells its delicious foods supermarket-style.

✚ blll ✉ Via dello Studio 26r ☎ 055 282 701 🚌 In the pedestrian zone

PORTA ROMANA
At the far end of the Boboli Gardens is a traditional *gastronomia* selling a mouth-watering range of cheeses, cold meats, ready prepared dishes and other delights from several different counters.

✚ G8 ✉ Corner of Porta Romana and Via U Foscolo 🚌 11, 12, 13, 36, 37, 68

I SAPORI DEL CHIANTI
A pretty shop with an excellent range of wines, including first-class Chianti and other Tuscan specialities.

✚ blll ✉ Via dei Servi 10r ☎ 055 238 2071 🚌 14, 23

SARTONI
A traditional baker that specialises in filled *focaccia* – great for picnics or snacks.

✚ blll ✉ Via dei Cerchi 34 ☎ 055 212 570 🚌 In the pedestrian zone

LA SORGENTE DELLE DELIZIE
Wines plus Italian candy and cookies.

✚ bll ✉ Via Cavour 30a ☎ 055 212 855 🚌 1, 7, 33

STANDA
Italy's only supermarket chain of any size. Cheap, but not always pleasant, it is worth checking out for the cultural experience. The olive oils and wines are good.

✚ clll ✉ Via Pietrapana 42 ☎ 055 234 7856 🚌 B

HOLY WINE & MORE
Trebbiano and Malvasia grapes are used to make *vin santo* (holy wine), which has a concentrated flavour and is about 14 per cent alcohol by volume. The grapes are semi-dried and made into wine, which is aged in small barrels for a number of years before bottling. It is drunk as a dessert wine – sometimes instead of dessert, when you use it to dunk hard, dry *biscotti di Prato* (also known as *cantuccini*).

Chianti gets its name from the region in which it is made. Sangiovese grapes are harvested in October, pressed and then the juice and skins of the grapes are fermented for about 15 days, after which the juice alone is given a second fermentation. In spring the wine is matured in wooden casks. *Chianti Classico* is usually regarded as the best of the seven types of Chianti. This is produced in the eponymous region north of Siena. Wines of the Chianti Classico Consortium bear the symbol of the *Gallo Nero* (black cockerel). The most famous Tuscan reds are made with Sangiovese grapes, including *Brunello di Montalcino* and *Vino Nobile di Montepulciano*. *Sassicaia*, made from Cabernet Sauvignon grapes, is also good.

Leather, Gloves & Shoes

SHOE CITY

The Florentines are justly famed for making superb shoes. As a testament to the historical importance of the industry in the city's economy, one of the main streets in Florence is named after the shoemakers (*Calzaiuoli*). The range of shoes available is vast, from the pinnacle of international chic to the value-for-money styles for sale in the market of San Lorenzo. The classiest leather shops are around the elegant Via de' Tornabuoni, while huge showrooms in the leather 'factories' in the Santa Croce area accommodate bus loads of tourists. The San Lorenzo market also has many stalls selling handbags, belts and jackets of varying degrees of quality. There are bargains to be had, but pitfalls too. The *vero cuoio* (genuine leather) sign refers only to the piece to which it is attached, which may be only a small proportion of the item.

LEATHER

IL BISONTE
Classic, top-class leather luggage and shoulder bags. Prices match the quality.
➕ alII ✉ Via del Parione 11 ☎ 055 211 976 🚌 C

CELLERINI
Elegant and sophisticated bags of outstanding quality. Styles tend to be fairly traditional.
➕ alII ✉ Via del Sole ☎ 055 282 533 🚌 36, 37

FURLA
Chic, handsomely designed bags and belts at prices that are less astronomic than elsewhere.
➕ bIII ✉ Via de' Tosinghi 5r ☎ 055 281 416 🚌 In the pedestrian zone

LEONCINI
This is famous for classic bags and belts made in a workshop on Via Palazzuolo.
➕ bII ✉ Via Ginori 13r (near Palazzo Medici-Riccardi) ☎ 055 282 533 🚌 1, 6, 7

MADOVA GLOVES
A staggering array of fine gloves lined with silk, cashmere and fur. Family run; established in 1919.
➕ aIV ✉ Via Guicciardini 1r ☎ 055 239 6526 🚌 B

MERCATO SAN LORENZO
Check out the San Lorenzo market glove stands for enchanting sheepskin mittens for children and more.
➕ bII ✉ Piazza San Lorenzo 🚌 In the pedestrian zone

MISURI
One of the best Santa Croce area leather factories.
➕ clV ✉ Piazza Santa Croce 20r ☎ 055 240 995 🚌 23

PAOLO CASALINI
A tiny workshop selling beautiful small leather goods, especially boxes.
➕ alII ✉ Via del Moro 44r ☎ 055 289 100 🚌 6, 11

SHOES

B&C
It's worth the slight detour (it's near Palazzo Pitti) for this huge range of men's, women's and children's shoes – all at good prices.
➕ H7 ✉ Via Romana 111r ☎ 055 229 8237 🚌 12, 13

FAUSTO SANTINI
Fashionable shoes in trendy, minimalist styles.
➕ bIII ✉ Via dei Calzaiuoli 95r ☎ 055 239 8536 🚌 In the pedestrian zone

FRATELLI ROSSETTI
Beautiful shoes in classic Italian styles.
➕ bIII ✉ Piazza della Repubblica 43–45r ☎ 055 216 656 🚌 In pedestrian zone

LILY OF FLORENCE
Affordable shoes in classic styles, aimed at tourists.
➕ aIV ✉ Via Guicciardini 2r ☎ 055 294 748 🚌 22, 23

SALVATORE FERRAGAMO
Designer shoes in the Palazzo Spini Feroni, which has a museum of shoes (➤ 53).
➕ aIV ✉ Via de' Tornabuoni 14r ☎ 055 292 123 🚌 6, 11, C

Gold & Jewellery

BOTTEGA ORAFA PENKO
Master goldsmith Paolo Penco makes jewellery to order using techniques from the Renaissance.
➕ alll ✉ Via F Zannetti 14 ☎ 055 211 661 🚌 22

BULGARI
Florence's branch of the world-famous fashion jeweller and watchmaker.
➕ alll ✉ Via de' Tornabuoni 61 ☎ 055 239 6786 🚌 6, 11, 36, 37

FIORI DEL TEMPO
In this tiny shop, a brother-and-sister team make exquisite reproductions of Medici jewels using semi-precious stones such as aquamarines and garnets. In place of gold, gilded brass gives a sense of antiquity, and makes these lovely, unusual and very Florentine jewels decidedly affordable.
➕ blll ✉ Via dei Pucci 3a ☎ 055 239 6443 🚌 Short walk from San Lorenzo

FREON
Quirky, stylish pieces made of unusual materials in a modern idiom that draws upon historical inspiration, notably art nouveau.
➕ alV ✉ Via Guicciardini 118r ☎ 055 239 6504 🚌 6, C, B

THE GOLD CORNER
This frequent tour group stop in Piazza Sante Croce sells gold by weight along with typical Italian cameos and coral.
➕ clV ✉ Piazza Santa Croce 15r ☎ 055 241 971; fax: 055 247 8437 🚌 23

PARSIFAL
An unusual selection of jewellery, including a small range of Renaissance styles as well as many eye-catching, affordable aluminium pieces.
➕ alll ✉ Via della Spada 28r ☎ 055 288 610 🚌 6, 11

RICCI E BARONI
Jewellery made of gold, diamonds and other precious stones in classic styles you find on the Ponte Vecchio, but at more competitive prices. The showroom is in the same fabulous Palazzo Frescobaldi as the workshop.
➕ alV ✉ Via Santo Spirito 11 ☎ 055 289 327 🚌 6, 11

TIME OUT
Beautiful second-hand watches ranging from antique erotic pocket watches to gentlemen's dress watches. There is also a wonderful collection of gold jewellery from the 1920s and 1940s as well as second-hand Tiffany cufflinks and 1920s cigar cutters.
➕ blV ✉ Via dei Bardi 70r ☎ 055 213 111 🚌 B, C

UFFIZI GALLERY SHOP
The Uffizi Gallery shop sells a small collection of jewellery modelled exactly on pieces worn in portraits in the Uffizi's collection.
➕ blV ✉ Loggiato degli Uffizi 6 ☎ 055 238 8651 🕐 Tue–Sun 9–7 (last admission 30 minutes before closing). Closed May 1 🚶 In the pedestrian zone

GOLD FACTS

A dazzling array of gold is for sale all over Florence, most notably on the Ponte Vecchio: in 1593 Ferdinand I decreed that only goldsmiths and jewellers should work there and it has remained that way ever since. The gold sold in Florence is 18 carat, often expressed as a rather confusing 750 per cent (with the per cent sign actually referring to 1000). Gold is also found – at somewhat lower prices – in the Santa Croce area, where, in accordance with tradition, all gold jewellery and other items are sold by weight.

Fashion for All

STYLISH CITY

One of Florence's many claims to fame is as the headquarters of Gucci. It was also in Florence, in 1927, that Salvatore Ferragamo established himself, after having made his reputation in Hollywood crafting shoes for the likes of Greta Garbo, Vivien Leigh, Gloria Swanson and the gladiators in Cecil B de Mille costume epics. This family still administers a fashion empire, producing accessories and clothes as well as the trademark shoes. Ties are also for sale in Florence at remarkably good prices. The market of San Lorenzo is the cheapest place, but even on the Ponte Vecchio the prices are agreeable!

COIN

A huge clothing and design emporium with a vast range of goods at reasonable prices on the Via dei Calzaiuoli. Open on Sunday.

🔒 bIII 🖂 Via dei Calzaiuoli 56r ☎ 055 280 531 🖵 In the pedestrian zone

DIADORA

An excellent place to buy an authentic Italian football shirt, prized among teenagers.

🔒 bIII 🖂 Via de' Tosinghi 8–10r ☎ 055 215 696 🖵 In the pedestrian zone

EMILIO CAVALLINI

A wonderfully wacky collection of socks and hosiery.

🔒 aIII 🖂 Via della Vigna Nuova 52r ☎ 055 238 2789 🖵 C

EMILIO PUCCI

A renowned Florentine fashion house created in 1950 by Marquis Emilio Pucci. The *haute couture* is shown in the Palazzo dei Pucci, the ready-to-wear in shops on Via della Vigna Nuova and Via Ricasoli.

🔒 aIII 🖂 Via della Vigna Nuova 97–99r ☎ 055 294 028 🖵 In the pedestrian zone; 🔒 bIII 🖂 Via Ricasoli 36r ☎ 055 287 622 🖵 In the pedestrian zone

ERMENEGILDO ZEGNA

An incredibly trendy menswear shop for the seriously cool and seriously rich.

🔒 aIII 🖂 Piazza Rucellai 4–7r ☎ 055 283 011 🖵 In the pedestrian zone

GUCCI

A predictably elegant and pricey shop; headquarters of the Gucci empire.

🔒 aIII 🖂 Via de' Tornabuoni 73r ☎ 055 264 011 🖵 6, 11

HERMÈS

The biggest and best-equipped branch of this Paris-based designer in Italy.

🔒 aIII 🖂 Piazza Antinori 6r ☎ 055 238 1004 🖵 1, 6, 12, 22

MARCELLA

An elegant clothes shop with an extremely well-selected collection of women's clothes, lingerie and accessories, suitable for all ages. Also has beautiful clothes for men, from formal suits to well-cut casual shirts.

🔒 bIII 🖂 Via dei Pecori 6r ☎ 055 213 162 🖵 In the pedestrian zone

MARINA LOFT

A selection of elegant but affordable Italian designer lines in a good range of sizes. The shop, near the Duomo, is spacious and the service courteous.

🔒 bIII 🖂 Via Martelli 29r ☎ 055 218 816 🖵 In the pedestrian zone

MAX & CO

The trendy branch of Max Mara; sells well-designed high-fashion pieces to a mainly teenage clientele, but with a range of versatile, classic items as well.

🔒 bIII 🖂 Via dei Calzaiuoli 89r ☎ 055 228 8656 🖵 In the pedestrian zone

MAX MARA

Classic elegance takes precedence over ostentation; clothes are of superb quality and beautifully tailored – yet at reasonable prices.

✚ bIII ✉ Via dei Pecori 23 ☎ 055 287 761 🚌 In the pedestrian zone

MERCATO DELLE CASCINE

The biggest of Florence's markets takes place every Tuesday morning in the Parco delle Cascine, a large park on the banks of the Arno, to the west of the city. Among its hundreds of stalls are many selling inexpensive clothes, plus shoes, leather goods and some second-hand clothes.

✚ G6 ✉ Viale Abramo Lincoln, Parco delle Cascine 🕐 Tue 7AM–1:30PM 🚌 1, 9, 12

MERCATO SAN LORENZO

In the San Lorenzo market plenty of clothes fall into the value category. In addition to fun T-shirts, there are lambswool and angora sweaters at reasonable prices. Also good for inexpensive scarves and ties.

✚ bII ✉ Piazza San Lorenzo 🚌 In the pedestrian zone

PATTAYA DUE

This discount shop offers designer clothes and accessories for men and women at up to 50 per cent off. A must for designer devotees.

✚ bII ✉ Via Cavour 51r ☎ 055 210 151 🚌 In the pedestrian zone

PRADA

The world's favourite Italian fashion house of the moment. The headquarters are in Milan but there's a good range of clothes, shoes, bags and accessories in this branch.

✚ aIII ✉ Via de' Tornabuoni 67r ☎ 055 283 439 🚌 6, 11, 36, 37

PRINCIPE

A large shop selling practical, sensible clothes for men, women and children.

✚ aIII ✉ Via degli Strozzi 29r ☎ 055 292 764 🚌 In the pedestrian zone

QUELLE TRE

Well-tailored, original clothes that are chic and aimed at younger women.

✚ bIII ✉ Via dei Pucci 43r ☎ 055 293 284 🚌 1, 6, 7

LA RINASCENTE

This is one of the newest branches of this Italian department store. The clothes are safe rather than exciting but prices are good and there's the odd find to be made. There are also perfumery, lingerie and other departments for those who like everything under one roof.

✚ C8 ✉ Piazza della Repubblica 🚌 In the pedestrian zone

STILNUOVO

The ultimate tie shop sells a wide selection of ties custom-made from a colourful selection of silks.

✚ bIII ✉ Via Dante Alighieri 8r ☎ 055 238 1567 🚌 In the pedestrian zone

DISTRICTS FOR CLOTHES SHOPPING

Armani, Gucci, Versace, Ferragamo, Trussardi and Valentino are in the district of the Via de' Tornabuoni and the Via della Vigna Nuova. The area around Piazza della Repubblica and Via dei Calzaiuoli has a good range of expensive clothes shops, including Max Mara and Marcella. In the streets east of Via dei Calzaiuoli, in particular Via del Corso, there are many mid-range fashion boutiques. The areas around Santa Croce and San Lorenzo sell bargain fashions to the tourist market.

Linens, Fabrics & Furnishings

HOPE CHEST

Although patterns of marriage in Italy have changed drastically in the last 20 years, with people statistically less and less likely to get married (and even less likely to have children), the idea of the *coreddo* (trousseau) persists, especially in the south, and a number of shops in Florence sell the kinds of linens that such a trousseau demands. Often the same shops sell baby clothes and women's underwear in irresistible styles.

CASA NEL CORTILE

An excellent selection of papers, fabrics and objects for the home.
🕂 dIII ✉ Via Antonio Scialoia 29r ☎ 055 234 6095 🚌 6, 8

CIRRI

Beautifully finished lace handkerchiefs and embroidered pieces for men and women. There is also a large collection of extremely expensive baby clothes and layette items as well as lacy underwear for women. Italians typically expect to spend lavishly on these things and they are certainly not cheap.
🕂 bIV ✉ Via Por Santa Maria 38–40r ☎ 055 239 6593 🚌 In the pedestrian zone

CONTROLUCE

The shop specialises in lighting but it also carries a good range of gift ideas and other items for the home.
🕂 aIII ✉ Via della Vigna Nuova 89r ☎ 055 239 8871 🚌 6, 11

LORETTA CAPONI

Deliciously feminine linens, nightclothes and lingerie for mother and daughter. All the components of a traditional trousseau are here, including exquisite bed linen.
🕂 aIII ✉ Piazza Antinori 4r ☎ 055 213 668 🚌 6, 11, 36, 37

MERCATO NUOVO

This market (with *Il Porcellino*), not the San Lorenzo market, is the best place to look for cheap tablecloths, linens and lace. You'll find an impressive variety of modern and more traditional designs.
🕂 bIII ✉ Piazza Mercato Nuovo 🚌 In the pedestrian zone

PASSAMANERIA TOSCANA FIRENZE

This shop sells a comprehensive range of furnishing fabrics, brocades, tassels and other trimmings as well as finished goods such as cushions and footstools. The colours and textures are rich and sensuous, bordering on the abandoned. A treat for anyone with an interest in fabric and furnishing.
🕂 bII ✉ Piazza San Lorenzo 12r ☎ Fax: 055 239 6389 🚌 In the pedestrian zone

PASSAMANERIA VALMAR

A compact shop that sells trims and finishings for fashion and upholstery.
🕂 bIII ✉ Via Porta Rossa 53r ☎ 055 284 493 🚌 In the pedestrian zone

TAF

This shop specialises in trousseau articles, including high-quality hand-finished table and bed linens.
🕂 bIV ✉ Via Por Santa Maria 17r ☎ 055 239 6037 🚌 A, B (in the pedestrian zone)

VALLI

Fine dress fabrics as used by Dormeuil, Armani, Versace, Gianfranco Ferré and their ilk.
🕂 aIII ✉ Via Strozzi 4–6r ☎ 055 282 485 🚌 A (in the pedestrian zone)

Ceramics

CARNESECCHI

A huge emporium of Italian ceramics, particularly Deruta wares.

� alV ✉ Via Guicciardini 4r ☎ 055 239 8523 🚌 B, C

CERAMICHE ND DOLFI

If you're serious about buying ceramics, head out to Montelupo Fiorentino, southeast of the city, to this family-run producer where a whole range of house and garden objects are made and decorated by hand. Signor Dolfi will advise you himself.

🔲 Off map ✉ Via Toscoromagnola nord 1, Località Antinoro, Montelupo Fiorentino ☎ 0571 51264

COSE DEL PASSATO

An antiques shop specialising in vintage ceramics from Montelupo.

🔲 alll ✉ Via dei Fossi 3–5r ☎ 055 294 689 🚌 In the pedestrian zone

DISS

Charming, unpretentious rustic ceramics, including spotted peasant pots. There is also a selection of glass from Empoli.

🔲 H7 ✉ Piazza del Carmine 14r ☎ 055 292 186 🚌 B

FORNACCE POGGI

On the southern outskirts of Florence, this is the place for terracotta garden pots, oil vats and other things – all made with traditional methods in antique-shapes and forms.

🔲 Off map ✉ Via Imprunetana 16 ☎ 055 201 1077 🚌 Off the bus routes

MACHIAVELLI

At this tourist shop, near the Ponte Vecchio, highlights include fruit bowls made of rings of ceramic geese.

🔲 blV ✉ Via Por Santa Maria 39r ☎ 055 239 8586 🚌 In the pedestrian zone

MASTROCILIEGIA

Playful plates and mugs with huge, brightly coloured designs in a variety of styles.

🔲 L2 ✉ Piazza Mino 3, Fiesole ☎ 055 598 962 🚌 7

PAMPALONI

As well as ceramics, this *oggettistica* (high-quality gift shop aimed at the wedding-present market) has a good range of silverware and porcelain.

🔲 alV ✉ Borgo Santi Apostoli 47r ☎ 055 289 094 🚌 4

RICHARD GINORI

Florence's own porcelain designer. Also does dinner services to order with your family crest, a picture of your home or whatever else you want.

🔲 alll ✉ Via Rondinelli 17r ☎ 055 210 041 🚌 6, 11, 17

SGIBOLI TERRACOTTE

Pots here are designed, painted and fired in Florence by the family owners and are bought by Florentines as well as tourists. The delightful designs for house and garden come in majolica and unglazed terracotta – and at very good prices.

🔲 clll ✉ Via Sant'Egidio 4r ☎ 055 247 9713 🕐 Closed Mon morning 🚌 14, 23

POTTERY FACTS

Traditional Italian ceramics are *majolica* (pronounced maiolica), terracotta covered with a brilliant tin-based glaze. Arabic ceramics (which came to Italy via Spain) inspired pots made for the Medici court at Montelupo, near Florence, sold in a ceramics museum (➤ 21) there. Deruta in Umbria makes flowery designs in blue on white or yellow. Designs in turquoise on white are also much in evidence, as are rustic styles from Puglia. Tuscan peasant wares, white or yellow, splashed with green or blue spots, are increasingly popular. Among the best-known classic designs is Gran Faenza, with green, red and blue floral designs on a pale grey-blue background. All shops on this page offer shipping.

Stationery, Cards & Calendars

GIULIO GIANNINI E FIGLIO

The best-known of Florence's stationery shops, established in 1856, sells tasteful greeting cards and books bound in leather, as well as beautifully finished desktop paraphernalia, letter racks and pen holders, all covered with marbled paper.

🔀 alV ✉ Piazza Pitti 37r ☎ 055 212 621 🖃 B, C

MERCATO SAN LORENZO

There is a great variety of cheap stationery in the markets of Florence, especially the Mercato San Lorenzo. Look especially for calendars, with themes such as architecture or botanical prints, all remarkably inexpensive.

🔀 bII ✉ Piazza San Lorenzo 🖃 B (in the pedestrian zone)

IL PAPIRO

These shops in the centre of Florence sell excellent marbled paper goods in particularly pretty colours. These include little chests of drawers and tiny jewellery boxes.

🔀 bII ✉ Via Cavour 55r; Piazza del Duomo 24r; Lungarno Acciaiuoli 42r ☎ 055 215 262; 🔀 aIV/bIII ✉ Via dei Tavolini 13r ☎ 055 213 823

PINEIDER

Chic, expensive stationery and book bindings. One of the characteristic papers covering diaries and address books is decorated with great artists' signatures.

🔀 bIII ✉ Piazza della Signoria 13r ☎ 055 284 655 🔀 aIII ✉ Via de' Tornabuoni 76r ☎ 055 211 605 🖃 B (in the pedestrian zone)

SCRIPTORIUM

This shop draws on two great Florentine crafts – leather working and papermaking – to create objects of great beauty and refined taste that are almost too beautiful to be used. The plain paper books are notable, bound with exquisitely soft leather in subdued natural shades.

🔀 alV ✉ Piazza Pitti 6; 🔀 bIII ✉ Via dei Servi 5r ☎ 055 238 2272 🖃 B (in the pedestrian zone)

SORBI

A kiosk in the middle of Piazza della Signoria now in its third generation of ownership, this is the very best place in Florence to buy postcards. Save yourself many a frustrating hour and come here first to look for postcards, particularly those of the great art in Florence's museums and churches.

🔀 bIII ✉ Piazza della Signoria ☎ 055 294 554 🖃 B (in the pedestrian zone)

IL TORCHIO

As you walk into this shop, you are instantly aware that this is a place where things are made, not just a showroom. You can buy sheets of marbled paper or have it made up to suit your requirements. There are also ready-made marbled paper goods available.

🔀 bIV ✉ Via dei Bardi 17 ☎ 055 234 2862 🖃 B, C

MARBLED PAPER

The skill of marbling paper was brought to Florence from Venice, where it had been learned from the East in the 12th century. Today's Florentine paper goods range greatly in price and quality, but even the cheap goods are very attractive – and easily transported.

Antiques & Prints

ANTIK

If you're looking for something particularly unusual, this is the place to come.

✚ G7 ✉ Via dei Serragli 144 ☎ 055 220 687 🚍 6, 11, 36, 37, 68

ART NOUVEAU

Period jewellery in all sorts of styles (mainly 20th century) with a range of prices that should suit most pockets.

✚ aIII ✉ Via della Scala 43a ☎ 055 284 539 🚍 17, 22, 29, 30, 64, 65

BACCANI

A beautiful shop, established in 1903. The old interior is filled with prints, engravings, paintings and old maps. Prices vary from very reasonable to very expensive.

✚ aIII ✉ Via della Vigna Nuova 75r ☎ 055 214 467 🚍 A, B

BOTTEGA DELLE STAMPE

Framed and unframed antique or art-nouveau prints (known in Italian as Liberty). Elegant.

✚ aIV ✉ Borgo San Jacopo 56r ☎ 055 295 396 🚍 C

CASTORINA

Carved and decorated wood, including friezes, tables, chairs and other items, both painted and lacquered furniture.

✚ aIV ✉ Via Santo Spirito 15r ☎ 055 212 885 🚍 11, C

HALL INTERNATIONAL

The building that houses this shop is a treat in itself: an art-nouveau townhouse. You'll find very expensive antiques.

✚ H6 ✉ Borgo Ognissanti 26 ☎ 055 287 428 🚍 9, C

LEONARDO SARUBBI

A delightfully shabby cavern of a shop near the Palazzo Pitti selling reasonably priced reproductions of antique prints including many 17th- and 18th-century views of Florence and botanical prints. Relaxed and casual.

✚ aIV ✉ Sdrucciolo de' Pitti 11r ☎ 055 238 1850 🚍 B, C

MERCATO DELLE PULCI

Bric-a-brac and junk stands in Piazza dei Ciompi sell all manner of bits and pieces. On the last Sunday in every month you'll find a full-scale flea market. A great place to browse, with the odd bargain to be had among a lot of very pricey junk.

✚ cIII ✉ Piazza dei Ciompi 🚍 B

STUDIO PUCK

Great selection of historic prints, water-coloured by hand, to buy framed or unframed.

✚ aIV ✉ Via dello Sprone 12r ☎ 055 280 954 🚍 3, 13, 32

VANDA NENCIONI

Pretty gilded frames, as well as period and modern prints.

✚ bIII ✉ Via della Condotta 36r ☎ 055 215 345 🚍 In the pedestrian zone

WHAT IS AN ANTIQUE?

Under Italian law an antique need not be old, but need only be made of old materials. For this reason, what would be called reproduction elsewhere is labelled as an antique in Italy.

Hundreds of shops all over Florence sell antiques, from the glamorous international emporia on Borgo Ognissanti to the flea market in Piazza dei Ciompi – there are whole streets of them. The most important include Borgo Ognissanti (✚ aIII) and Via Maggio (✚ aIV), for very expensive antiques gorgeously displayed; and streets such as Via dei Serragli (✚ H7) in the Oltrarno area, where considerably less grand shops are scattered among the artisans' workshops.

Bars by Night

Going out in Florence doesn't have to mean actually going anywhere. In summer, a particularly enjoyable and popular way of spending time after dinner is to stroll through the streets of the historic centre, stopping off for an ice cream or a drink at a bar. You'll see plenty of groups of Italians of all ages doing the same thing.

DRINKING LAWS

The legal age for buying alcohol in bars or shops is 18. Opening times for licensed premises are not set, although there are restrictions before, during and after some football matches. Laws against drinking and driving are firmly enforced.

CABIRIA

A trendy, bohemian bar in Piazza Santo Spirito with outdoor seating. This is Florence's answer to a Left-Bank Paris café. Uncharacteristically for Italy, people linger over their coffees, snacks and beer. Food is served at all times of the day and night and there are paintings on the walls inside for sale.

➕ aIV ✉ Piazza Santo Spirito ☎ 055 215 732 🕔 Closed Tue 🚍 B

CAFFÈ NOTTE

Pleasantly low-key bar situated close to Piazza Santo Spirito; much frequented by the artists and artisans who live and work in the Oltrarno area. Stays open until 2AM.

➕ H7 ✉ Via delle Caldaie 28r ☎ 055 223 067 🕔 Closed Mon 🚍 B

CAFFÈ RICCHI

This trendy Oltrarno bar is a good place to have coffee during the day, but it really only comes alive at night, especially in summer, when you can sit outside.

➕ aIV ✉ Piazza Santo Spirito 9r ☎ 055 215 864 🕔 Mon–Sat 7AM–1AM 🚍 B

HARRY'S BAR

This trendy bar is the only example of a true American-style bar in Florence, and the best place for elegant cocktails. The food is international and very good; you can also get a first-class hamburger. The service is speedy and exemplary.

On the banks of the River Arno.

➕ aIII ✉ Lungarno Vespucci 22r ☎ 055 239 6700 🕔 Closed Sun 🚍 C

HEMINGWAY

Chic, funky café and bar with light meals, great cocktails, speciality teas, fine coffees and chocolates, just off Piazza del Carmine.

➕ H7 ✉ Piazza Piattellina 9r ☎ 055 284 781 🕔 Mon–Sat 11–8 🚍 B

REX CAFFÈ

A heavy-drinking and billiards-playing kind of place. Very sociable and frequented by the 25–35 age group, with Florentines and foreigners mixing freely and convivially. Open until 1AM.

➕ cIII ✉ Via Fiesolana 23r ☎ 055 248 0331 🚍 14, 23, 71

SATANASSA BAR

A popular and centrally located gay bar. Air-conditioned – a real bonus in summer.

➕ cIII ✉ Via dei Pandolfini 26; 1st floor ☎ 055 243 356 🚍 14

ZOE

A sleek, brightly coloured design sets the atmosphere. There is a daily happy 'hour' from 6 to 9PM.

➕ J7 ✉ Via dei Renai 13r ☎ 055 243 111 🕔 8AM–1AM 🚍 C, 23, 71

Clubs & Discos

ANDROMEDA

This central and perennially popular disco appeals to locals and visitors alike, especially those under 25.

🔢 bIII ✉ Via dei Cimatori 13 ☎ 055 292 002 🕐 Closed Sun 🚌 A

LA DOLCE VITA

The chosen haunt of the beautiful people. In summer the lively action often spills out into the piazza, so you can enjoy the spectacle as a passerby.

🔢 H7 ✉ Piazza del Carmine ☎ 055 284 595 🕐 Closed Sun 🚌 B

MARACANA

A Brazilian club in an old theatre, with shows and live music. Go early for a full dinner; later on, try the tropically flavoured pizza.

🔢 all ✉ Via Faenza 4 ☎ 055 210 298 🚌 Close to the railway station

MARAMAO

A Mercato Sant'Ambrogio bar and restaurant that never sleeps, with breakfast, lunch and dinner at good prices and interesting and varied live music. Very popular with the Florentines – always a good sign. In summer the action moves outside to the piazza.

🔢 cIII ✉ Via dei Macci 79r ☎ 055 244 341 🚌 14

MECCANÒ

A chic club where you can dance into the small hours.

🔢 F5 ✉ Via degli Olmi 1 ☎ 055 331 371 🚌 1, 2, 9, 12, 26, 27

SPACE ELECTRONIC

Upstairs you'll find a vast dance floor, where a huge variety of music is played, from up-to-the-minute hits to 1950s and 60s classics. Downstairs there is karaoke and room to chat. At Easter and in June and July this club caters extensively to groups of young tourists, who have a tendency to leave, Cinderella fashion, at midnight.

🔢 alII ✉ Via Palazzuolo 37 ☎ 055 293 082 🚌 5 minutes' walk from the station

TABASCO 1

A very popular gay disco, not far from the Piazza della Signoria.

🔢 bIII ✉ Piazzetta Santa Cecilia 3r ☎ 055 213 000 🕐 Closed Mon 🚌 In the pedestrian zone

TENAX

Trendy and up-to-date music and a huge dance floor; very popular with both Florentines and foreigners.

🔢 D3 ✉ Via Pratese 47 ☎ 055 308 160 🕐 Closed Mon and Wed 🚌 Towards the airport

YAB

This is one of Florence's most central discos, which means it is often full of young visitors to the city. Music and fashions here are always up-to-the-minute.

🔢 alII ✉ Via Sassetti 5r ☎ 055 215 160 🕐 Closed Wed, Sun 🚌 A

LATE START

Florentine clubs start and end late. The first trickle of action is usually about 10:30PM or 11PM. Closing time is between 3AM and 5AM. The entrance fee is generally around 12.50 euros/L25,000 and includes one drink.

Opera & Classical Music

OPERA'S REBIRTH

Florence is one of the birthplaces of opera. At the end of the 16th century, a group of dilettanti attempted to re-create the musical glories of ancient Greek theatre. The first performance, Jacopo Peri's *Euridice*, was held in the amphitheatre of the Giardino di Boboli (➤ 29).

FESTIVALS

ESTATE FIESOLANA

A season of music, opera and ballet known as the Sunset Concerts, primarily in the open-air Roman Theatre in Fiesole (➤ 20), from late June to August. Performances are by Tuscan and Italian groups with the occasional visitor from abroad. The main attraction is chamber and symphonic music, hosted by The Badia Fiesolana. Other events are staged in Santa Croce or the courtyard of the Palazzo Pitti. The concerts are an unbeatable experience.
Fondazione Toscana Spettacolo ✚ H6 ✉ Via Luigi Alamanni 41 ☎ 055 21985;
Roman Theatre ✚ Off map ✉ Via Marini 🚌 7;
Box Office ✚ all ✉ Via Alamanni 39 ☎ 055 210 804

MAGGIO MUSICALE FIORENTINO

This major musical festival held between May and early July includes opera and ballet as well as orchestral concerts and chamber music. It has its own orchestra, chorus and ballet troupe. The main venue is the Teatro Comunale; the Teatro della Pergola and the Teatro Verdi are used for more intimate recitals. The main box office is the Teatro Comunale (➤ this page).

VENUES

PALAZZO DEI CONGRESSI

The main venue from October to June for the classical music company, *Musicus Concertus*.
✚ al ✉ Viale Filippo Strozzi ☎ 055 26025 (Musicus Concertus ☎ 055 287 347)

SANTA MARIA DEI RICCI

Many organ recitals are held in this church.
✚ bIII ✉ Via del Corso 🚌 A (in the pedestrian zone)

TEATRO COMUNALE

The largest of Florence's concert halls – the main venue of the Maggio Musicale and the festival's box office – also has its own classical season from mid-September to December. The opera season then begins, finishing mid-January and from then until April symphony concerts are held. The Ridotto or Piccolo is the Teatro Comunale's smaller auditorium.
✚ G6 ✉ Corso Italia 16 ☎ 055 27791/055 211 158 🚌 C

TEATRO DELLA PERGOLA

An important venue for classical music in Florence, with some Maggio Musicale and Estate Fiesolana concerts held here. From October to April the Amici della Musica organise Saturday afternoon concerts here.
✚ cIII ✉ Via della Pergola 12 ☎ 055 247 9651 🚌 23, 71

TEATRO VERDI

This theatre puts on drama, ballet and opera from January to April.
✚ dIV ✉ Via Ghibellina 101 ☎ 055 239 6242 🚌 14

Live Music

AUDITORIUM FLOG

This is probably the best known of Florence's live music venues, where music of all kinds is performed; regular themed disco evenings.
✚ H4 ✉ Via Mercati 24b
☎ 055 487145 🚌 4

IL BARRETTO

A small, intimate and fashionable bar, frequented by professionals, serving excellent drinks in congenial surroundings with civilised live piano music in the background.
✚ allI ✉ Via del Parione 50r
☎ 055 294 122 🚌 C

IL CAFFÈ

This pretty bar–café is a good place for coffee during the day, but in the evening it has live music – mostly jazz and blues – and serves light meals.
✚ alV ✉ Piazza Pitti 9r
☎ 055 239 6241 🕐 Daily 11AM–2AM

CHIODSO FISSO CLUB

Popular, well-established wine bar run by a dedicated folk music enthusiast. You will find Italian folk music at its best in this candlelit setting. Very centrally located.
✚ bIII ✉ Via Dante Alighieri 16r ☎ 055 238 1290 🚌 A (in the pedestrian zone)

CITTÀ DI FIRENZE

An elegant riverside restaurant with an American-style bar, where you can eat and drink to the accompaniment of live piano music.
✚ alII ✉ Lungarno Corsini 4
☎ 055 217706 🚌 C

DU MONDE

A wonderfully civilised venue for light jazz music in the Oltrarno. Come here to enjoy a candlelit dinner with piano music. Later, settle down for some wonderful jazz. Very popular, so book ahead.
✚ J7 ✉ Via di San Niccolò 103r ☎ 055 234 4953
🕐 Closed Mon 🚌 13, 23, 71

GIRASOL

Florentines have a passion for Latin American bars. This is the best, with live and recorded Cuban, Caribbean and other Latin-American music.
✚ H4/5 ✉ Via del Romito 1r
☎ 055 474 948 🕐 Tue–Sun until 2:30AM 🚌 14

H202

A central club close to Santa Croce where you can hear local bands playing jazz, rock, blues and reggae.
✚ cIII ✉ Via Ghibellina 47r
☎ 055 243 239 🕐 Closed Mon 🚌 14, A

JAZZ CLUB

Another very popular venue among real jazz aficionados. Although technically a private club, it is very easy to become a member (► panel).
✚ cIII ✉ Via Nuova dei Caccini 3 ☎ 055 247 9700
🕐 Closed Mon 🚌 14, 23, 71

CLUBBING ITALIAN STYLE

Many clubs and music venues (and even a few bars and restaurants) are officially private clubs or *associazione culturale*. This doesn't mean that visitors are unwelcome but rather that it's easier for them to get a licence as a club than as a public *locale*. It's easy to become a member; you may be charged a euro or a few thousand lire over and above the official entry price, but it's still worth doing so even if you're only going to use your membership once. Many clubs actually have free membership. All you need to do is fill in your name, address, date of birth and sometimes occupation on a form and you'll be presented with a membership card.

Sport

FOOTBALL IS ALL

Many Florentines take much more immediate pride in their football team than in their artistic heritage. 'I Viola' (The Purples) is the familiar way of referring to La Fiorentina. Though not up with AC Milan and Lazio, the team has a more than respectable reputation, usually hanging on in Serie A throughout the season and securing a place in the Champions' League. They play at the Stadio Artemio Franchi on Sundays from August to May. You can book in advance (☎ 055 507 2245) to join the 40,000 or more fans cheering on the lads in lavender.

SPECTATOR SPORTS

FOOTBALL

The magnificent Stadio Franchi, also known as Stadio Comunale or the Palazzo dello Sport, is where I Viola play football.
✚ L5 ⊠ 17

POLO

A polo tournament is held annually in Florence in June. On other occasions polo is played in the Piazza Santa Croce; however, the usual location is the racecourse – the Ippodromo delle Muline – in the park of Le Cascine (➤ 58).
✚ G6 ⊠ Ippodromo delle Muline, Le Cascine ☎ 055 422 6076

PARTICIPATORY SPORTS

BOWLING
BOWLING PALASPORT
Near the railway station.
✚ all ⊠ Via Faenza 71 ☎ 055 238 1380

CANOEING
SOCIETA CANOTTIERI COMUNALI
Hire a canoe and paddle your way along the Arno.
✚ K7 ⊠ Lungarno Ferrucci 6 ☎ 055 681 2649

EXERCISE
GYMNASIUM
Fairly good weights, but not the latest technology.
✚ allI ⊠ Via Palazzuolo 49r ☎ 055 293 308

SQUASH
CENTRO SQUASH
✚ D6 ⊠ Via Empoli 16 ☎ 055 732 3055

SWIMMING
PISCINA COMUNALE BELLARIVA
An outdoor Olympic swimming pool with a smaller one for children in pleasant shady gardens east of the city.
✚ L7 ⊠ Lungarno Colombo 6 ☎ 055 677 521 ⏰ Jun–Sep 🚌 14

PISCINA LE PAVONIERE
Most popular (used by Florentines but also visitors) outdoor pool in Florence, in Le Cascine (➤ 58).
✚ G6 ⊠ Le Cascine ☎ 055 333 979 ⏰ Jun–Sep 🚌 17 to Piazza Vittorio Veneto and then D

ZODIAC
A huge complex with four swimming pools (two indoor), pleasant gardens and a bar. Take the N2 to La Certosa and follow the signs for Tavernuzze, just outside Florence.
✚ Off map to south ⊠ Via Grandi 2 ☎ 055 202 2888 🚌 37

TENNIS
CIRCOLO CARRAIA
On the hill leading up to San Miniato. The floodlit outdoor courts get busy during lunchtimes and early evenings but are quieter in summer and during weekdays. Bring a racket.
✚ J7 ⊠ Via Monti alle Croci ☎ 055 234 6353

ZODIAC
See above.
✚ Off map to south ⊠ Via Grandi 2, Tavernuzze ☎ 055 202 2850

Pageants in Tuscany

AREZZO

GIOSTRA DEL SARACINO

This jousting tournament in Crusade-era costume takes place in the central square of Arezzo, the Piazza Grande. Two knights, representing the town's four *contrade* (districts), charge towards a wooden model of a Saracen, which they aim to hit while avoiding the attached cat of three tails that swings back and can unseat them. The other side do everything they legitimately can to unnerve the knight, including making a deafening noise. The winner gets a golden lance.

✠ Off map ✉ Piazza Grande, Arezzo ⏰ Last Sun in Aug and 1st Sun in Sep ⏳ 40 minutes' train journey from Florence ℹ Piazza della Stazione (☎ 0575 377 678)

FLORENCE

CALCIO IN COSTUME

A football game between four teams of men who wear their district's medieval colours. The games, played in Piazza Santa Croce according to somewhat archaic rules, are preceded by a long procession accompanied by drums and trumpets. The winning team is presented with a live cow.

✠ dIV ✉ Piazza Santa Croce ⏰ Late Jun ℹ Via Cavour 1r (☎ 055 290 832)

PISA

GIOCO DEL PONTE

A grand tug-of-war between the inhabitants of the north and the south of Pisa on the Ponte di Mezzo, which divides the city. Participants wear Renaissance costume, and some have period armour; everyone carries shields decorated with their district emblems. The aim is to push a hefty carriage over the bridge into the river.

✠ Off map ✉ Ponte di Mezzo ⏰ Last Sun in Jun ⏳ 1 hour's train journey from Florence

REGATA DI SAN RANIERI

Colourful boat races on the River Arno are preceded by pageantry and processions. At night the buildings along the river are illuminated by flaming torches.

✠ Off map ✉ River Arno, Pisa ⏰ Jun 17 ℹ Piazza della Stazione 11 (☎ 050 42291)

SIENA

CORSO DEL PALIO

The most famous pageant of all, Siena's Palio is a breakneck horse race in the Piazza del Campo, a tradition since 1283. The horses are blessed in the churches of the 17 *contrade*; the jockeys ride bareback, wearing their district colours. The winner takes the *palio* or banner.

✠ Off map ✉ Piazza del Campo ⏰ 2 Jul, 16 Aug ℹ Piazza del Campo 56 (☎ 0577 280 551)

MEDIEVAL MAYHEM

All towns of Tuscany go in for pageantry. Participants dress up in the medieval or Renaissance costumes of their particular district or town and parade through the streets, then join in an aggressive, often violent competition – football, jousting or horse racing – with tremendous gusto. Visitors watch – as much as they can as it's crowded and there's a lot of jostling. Everyone has a wonderful time and a great deal to eat afterwards.

Luxury Hotels

PRICES

Approximate prices for a double room per night:

Luxury	over 180 euros/L350,000
Moderate	up to 180 euros/L350,000
Budget	up to 103 euros/L200,000

RESERVATIONS

Peak season in Florence runs from February to October, but the city's hotels are almost invariably busy. Telephone, write or fax well in advance for a room (virtually all receptionists speak some English, French or German). Leave a credit card number or send an international money order for the first night's stay to be certain of the reservation.

BRUNELLESCHI

A modern 96-room hotel housed in a medieval tower in a peaceful location just behind the Via Calzaiuoli.

✚ bIII ✉ Piazza Santa Elisabetta 3 ☎ 055 27370; fax: 055 219 653; www.hotelbrunelleschi.it ▣ In the pedestrian zone

DELLA SIGNORIA

A modern 27-room hotel with views of the Ponte Vecchio from the upper floors.

✚ aIII ✉ Via delle Terme 1 ☎ 055 214 530; fax: 055 216101; www.hoteldellasignoria.com ▣ In the pedestrian zone

EXCELSIOR

The grandest hotel in Florence, but in a not-so-grand piazza. Some of the 172 rooms have a view of the River Arno, and there is a roof terrace.

✚ H6 ✉ Piazza Ognissanti 3 ☎ 055 264 201; fax: 055 210 278; www.starwood.com ▣ 9, C

HELVETIA E BRISTOL

An 18th-century hotel in a superb location near the Duomo. Each of the 52 rooms is decorated differently. All the rooms have rich furnishings, and some have antiques, too.

✚ aIII ✉ Via dei Pescioni 2 ☎ 055 287 814; fax: 055 288 353; www.charminghotels.it ▣ 6, 11, 36, 37

HOTEL J & J

Close to touristy Santa Croce, this is a quiet 20-room hotel in a 16th-century monastery, with a glamorous international clientele.

✚ cIII ✉ Via di Mezzo 20 ☎ 055 263 121; fax: 055 240 282; www.jandjhotel.com ▣ B

KRAFT

Some of the 80 rooms are traditional, others are modern in this quiet and comfortable hotel, which also has a small roof-top swimming pool and some terrific views.

✚ G6 ✉ Via Solferino 2 ☎ 055 284 273; fax: 055 239 8267; www.krafthotel.it ▣ C

PRINCIPE

A small, elegant hotel with an old-world feel and 20 air-conditioned, sound proof rooms, many with terraces overlooking the Arno.

✚ aIII ✉ Lungarno Vespucci 34 ☎ 055 284 848; fax: 055 283 458; www.hotelprincipe.com ▣ C

TORRE DI BELLOSGUARDO

There are stupendous views of Florence from this fabulous hotel in a 16th-century villa and a huge 14th-century tower. The 16 spacious rooms are elegantly decorated with antiques. Swimming pool.

✚ Off map to southwest ✉ Via Roti Michelozzi 2 ☎ 055 229 8145; fax: 055 229 008

VILLA CORA

A beautifully decorated 48-room villa with its own grounds outside the city (there is a free shuttle).

✚ H8 ✉ Viale Machiavelli 18 ☎ 055 298 451; fax: 055 229 086; www.villacora.com ▣ 12, 13, 38

Mid-Range Hotels

ANNALENA

In a Medici *palazzo* opposite the Boboli Gardens, this hotel once favoured by artists and writers has pretty rooms with old-fashioned decor. Some rooms have terraces and views.

H7 ✉ Via Romana 34 ☎ 055 229 600; fax: 055 222 403; www.hotelannalena.it 🚌 36, 37

APRILE

This former Medici home has 28 rooms in different styles, sizes and prices.

alll ✉ Via della Scala 6 ☎ 055 216 237; fax: 055 280 947 🚌 2, 17, 22

BALESTRI

Close to the River Arno, between the Uffizi and Santa Croce, with 46 comfortable rooms.

bIV ✉ Piazza Mentana 7 ☎ 055 214 743; fax: 055 239 8042; www.hotel-balestri.it/ 🚌 23, 71

BEACCI TORNABUONI

This hotel, on the top three floors of a 14th-century *palazzo*, has 28 rooms of varying quality.

alll ✉ Via de' Tornabuoni 3 ☎ 055 212 645; fax: 055 283 594; www.bhotel.it 🚌 6, 11, 36, 37

LE DUE FONTANE

Modern 57-room hotel in the delightful Piazza della Santissima Annunziata.

cII ✉ Piazza della Santissima Annunziata 14 ☎ 055 210 185; fax: 055 294461 🚌 6, 31, 32

IL GUELFO BIANCO

A hotel well adapted for business travellers. Thirty spacious, comfortable rooms in fresh colours.

bII ✉ Via Cavour 57r ☎ 055 288 330; fax: 055 295 203; www.ilguelfobianco.it 🚌 1, 7, 33

HERMITAGE

A well-known 29-room hotel overlooking the Ponte Vecchio.

bIV ✉ Vicolo Marzio 1, Piazza del Pesce ☎ 055 287 216; fax: 055 212 208; www.hermitagehotel.com 🚌 In the pedestrian zone

PORTA ROSSA

Good enough for Byron and Stendhal, this elegant, spacious hotel is in a 14th-century building close to the Ponte Vecchio and has 65 ensuite rooms and 12 without bathrooms.

alll ✉ Via Porta Rossa 19 ☎ 055 287 551; fax: 055 282 179 🚌 In the pedestrian zone

LA RESIDENZA

Traditional comfortable 24-room hotel on the top four floors of a 17th-century *palazzo* on the super-elegant Via de' Tornabuoni.

alll ✉ Via de' Tornabuoni 8 ☎ 055 218 684; fax: 055 284 197; www.laresidenzahotel.com 🚌 6, 11, 36, 37

VILLA AURORA

This hotel in Fiesole with a panorama of Florence offers exceptional value. Some of the 28 rooms have saunas and jacuzzis, many have terraces and all have air-conditioning. Central Florence is only a 20-minute bus ride away.

L2 ✉ Piazza Mino 39, Fiesole ☎ 055 59100; fax: 055 59587; www.villaaurora.it 🚌 7

WHICH ROOM?

The room with a view is a much sought-after thing. However, it can often come with street noise. Most Florentine hotels are in *palazzi* built around courtyards, so that the rooms with views face onto the street, while the ones looking over the courtyards are pleasantly quiet. You might like to forego the romance to ensure a good night's sleep.

Budget Hotels

If you arrive without a reservation, try the ITA (Informazioni Turistiche Alberghiere) office on the railway station concourse (🕒 Daily 8:30–9 ☎ 055 282 893). You'll pay a fee of 2–5 euros/L3,000–L10,000 for finding a room, depending on the category of hotel.

ABACO

Small, friendly family-run hotel close to the station and the Duomo. Nine clean, neat rooms and facilities for washing clothes and cooking.
✚ alll ✉ Via dei Banchi 1 ☎ (and fax) 055 238 1919 🚇 5 minutes' walk from the station

AZZI

Small, cheap, clean and in a quiet location close to the station. Twelve rooms (three ensuite).
✚ all ✉ Via Faenza 56 ☎ (and fax) 055 213 806 🚇 5 minutes' walk from station

BRETAGNA

Eighteen affordable rooms with views of the River Arno.
✚ alll ✉ Lungarno Corsini 6 ☎ 055 289 618; fax: 055 289 619 🚇 C

CRISTINA

A small, clean hotel in a medieval palace off a quiet street in the heart of Florence. Nine rooms (four ensuite).
✚ blll ✉ Via della Condotta 4 ☎ 055 214 484 🚇 In the pedestrian zone

FIRENZE

A 57-room modern hotel in a very quiet courtyard in the centre of Florence.
✚ blll ✉ Piazza dei Donati 4 ☎ 055 214 203; fax: 055 212 073 🚇 In the pedestrian zone

LOCANDA ORCHIDEA

Family-run hotel near the Duomo on the second floor of a 12th-century *palazzo*, with seven rooms.
✚ blll ✉ Borgo degli Albizi 11 ☎ (and fax) 055 248 0346 🚇 In the pedestrian zone

NUOVA ITALIA

Modern, clean 20-room hotel with friendly staff.
✚ all ✉ Via Faenza 26 ☎ 055 268 430; fax: 055 210 941 🚇 5 minutes' walk from the station

IL PERSEO

Clean and friendly, with 19 modern rooms (seven ensuite). Close to the railway station and the Duomo.
✚ blll ✉ Via Cerretani 1 ☎ 055 212 504; fax: 055 288 377 🚇 5 minutes' walk from the station.

POR SANTA MARIA

Eight-room, clean hotel by the Mercato Nuovo with great views of the Ponte Vecchio and Piazza della Signoria. Managed with loving pride and care. Take the lift to the third floor to find the reception desk. No breakfast.
✚ blll ✉ Via Calimaruzza 3 ☎ (and fax) 055 216 370 🚇 In the pedestrian zone

SORELLE BANDINI

Perfect for the more bohemian traveller, this *pensione* is on the top storey of a 1505 *palazzo* and has a fabulous loggia, ideal for picnics, and 10 huge rooms (one ensuite) with frescoed, slightly crumbling ceilings. The breakfast room looks over a panorama of terracotta-tile roofs to the Palazzo Pitti. The owners keep cats.
✚ alV ✉ Piazza Santo Spirito 9 ☎ 055 215 308; fax: 055 282 761 🚇 B, 36, 37

FLORENCE
travel facts

ESSENTIAL FACTS

Customs regulations
- EU nationals do not have to declare goods imported for their personal use.
- The limits for non-EU visitors are 200 cigarettes or 100 small cigars or 250g of tobacco; 1 litre of alcohol (over 22 per cent alcohol) or 2 litres of fortified wine; 50g of perfume.

Electricity
- Voltage is 220 volts and sockets take two round pins.

Etiquette
- Make the effort to speak some Italian: it will be appreciated.
- Shake hands on introduction and on leaving; once you know people better you can replace this with a kiss on each cheek.
- Use the polite form, *lei*, unless the other person uses *tu*.
- Always say *buon giorno* (hello) and *arrivederci* (goodbye) in shops.
- Italians do not get drunk in public.
- Smoking is common everywhere.

Money and credit cards
- American Express office ✉ Via Dante Alighieri 22r ☎ 055 50981
- Credit cards are widely accepted.
- Cash machines are now common.

National holidays
- 1 Jan: New Year's Day
- 6 Jan: Epiphany
- Easter Sunday
- Easter Monday
- 25 Apr: Liberation Day
- 1 May: Labour Day
- 15 Aug: Assumption
- 1 Nov: All Saints' Day
- 8 Dec: Immaculate Conception
- 25 Dec: Christmas Day
- 26 Dec: St Stephen's Day.

Opening times
- Banks: 8:30–1:20; in some instances also 2:45–4 Mon–Fri.
- Post offices: Mon–Fri 8:15–1:30; Sat 8:15–12:30.
- Shops: normally 8:30–1 and from 3 or 4 until 7 or 8; or 10–7.
- Museums: see individual entries.
- Churches: 7 or 8–12:30 and then from between 3 and 4 until 7:30. Main tourist attractions often stay open longer. No two are the same.

Places of worship
- Anglican: St Mark's ✉ Via Maggio 16 ☎ 055 294 764
- American Episcopal Church: St James' ✉ Via Rucellai 9 ☎ 055 294 417
- Lutheran ✉ Lungarno Torrigiani 11 ☎ 055 234 2775
- Synagogue ✉ Via Farini 4 ☎ 055 245 252/3
- Russian Orthodox ✉ Via Leone X 8 ☎ 055 490 148
- Greek Orthodox ✉ Viale Mattioli 76
- Mosque ✉ Piazza Scarlatti (off Via dei Geppi)

Street numbers
- One building can have two totally different numbers in Florence. The red lettering system is for shops, restaurants and businesses, while the blue system is for hotels or residences. Red numbers have an 'r' after them.

Student travellers
- Bring an ISIC card to get reductions on museum entry fees.
- If you intend to stay at youth hostels get a youth hostel card before leaving for Italy.

Toilets
- Italian toilets are improving but you can have some nasty shocks in the most unsuspected places.
- Expect to pay about 0.25 euros/L500 for toilets. Those away from

the main tourist areas are usually free.
- There are virtually no public toilets in Florence.
- Carry your own toilet paper or at least a packet of tissues.
- Most bars and cafés have toilets, which usually allow anybody to use them (although it's polite to have at least a drink).

Tourist information office
- Principal tourist office ☒ Via Cavour 1r ☎ 055 290 832/3; fax 055 276 0381

Women travellers
- Women are generally safe travelling alone or together in Florence.
- After dark avoid Le Cascine, Santa Maria Novella and the railway station.

PUBLIC TRANSPORT

Long-distance buses
- There are three main companies in Florence.
- Lazzi (► 7).
- SITA serves the south and east region ☒ Via Santa Caterina da Siena 15r ☎ 055 214 457 (Tuscany); 055 214 721 (national)
- CAP serves the region to the northeast of Florence, the Mugello ☒ Via Nazionale 13 ☎ 055 214 637

Bicycles
- Bicycles can be rented from Florence by Bike ☒ Via San Zanobi 120–122r ☎ 055 488 992

Cars
- The brochure *Florence Concierge* is available in hotels and tourist information offices.
- Car hire companies are in Borgo Ognissanti or Via Maso Finiguerra.
- Avis ☒ Borgo Ognissanti 128r

☎ 055 213 629
- Program ☒ Borgo Ognissanti 135r ☎ 055 282 916
- Tolls are payable on highways (*autostrade*).
- Most petrol stations in the country now take credit cards, but not all.
- Breakdown service: ACI ☒ Viale G Amendola 36, Florence ☎ 116/055 24861

Motorcycles
- Mopeds and motorcycles can be rented from Motorent ☒ Via San Zanobi 9r ☎ 055 490 113

Walking
- Walking is the best way of getting around the historic centre of Florence. However, it pays to use a bus sometimes to avoid blisters.

- For more transport information ► 6–7.

MEDIA & COMMUNICATIONS

Mail
- Main post office ☒ Via Pellicceria 8 ☎ 055 216.122/160 🕐 Mon–Sat 8:15–7
- There is another big post office at ☒ Via Pietrapiana 53–55 ☎ 055 27741 (same hours)
- Stamps (*francobolli*) can be bought from post offices or from tobacconists displaying a white T sign on a black or blue background.
- Post boxes are small, red and marked *Poste* or *Lettere*. The slot on the left is for addresses within the city and the slot on the right is for other destinations.

Telephones
- Public phones are orange. There are also a few telephone centres in the city (Via Cavour 21r 🕐 Daily 8AM–10PM)

- Few public telephones take coins. Phone cards (*carta* or *scheda* or *tessera telefonica*) are the most practical way to use a public phone.
- Directory enquiries ☎ 12
- International directory enquiries ☎ 176
- International operator ☎ 170; you can make reverse charge international calls by dialling 17200 followed by your country code (which will give you the operator).
- Cheap rate is all day Sunday and 9PM–8AM (national) on other days; 10PM–8AM (international).
- To call Italy from the UK, dial 00 followed by 39 (the code for Italy) then the number. To call the UK from Italy dial 00 44 then drop the first zero from the area code.
- Florence's area code (055) must be dialled even if you are calling from within Florence.

Press

- The Florentines' preferred newspaper is *La Nazione*, a national paper produced in Florence.
- You can buy foreign newspapers and magazines at the station and at Sorbi, in Piazza della Signoria.

EMERGENCIES

Telephone numbers

- Police, fire and ambulance ☎ 113
- Police headquarters (for passport problems, thefts, etc.) ☎ 055 49771

Embassies and consulates

- British Consulate ✉ Lungarno Corsini 2 ☎ 055 212 594
- US Consulate ✉ Lungarno Amerigo Vespucci 38 ☎ 055 239 8276

Lost property

- Lost property office ✉ Via Circondaria 19 ☎ 055 328 3942/367 943 🕔 9–noon. Closed Sun

- Report losses of passports to the police and other items to the Questura at Via Zara 2 ☎ 055 49771

Medicines and medical treatment

- EU nationals receive reduced cost medical treatment on production of the relevant document (E111 form for Britons). Private medical insurance is still advised.
- Medical emergencies ☎ 118
- First aid: Misericordia ambulance service ☎ 055 212 222
- Tourist medical service: has English-speaking doctors on 24-hour call ✉ Via Lorenzo il Magnifico 59 ☎ 055 475 4111
- Hospital: Santa Maria Nuova ✉ Piazza Santa Maria Nuova 1 ☎ 055 27581 Interpreters can be arranged free through Associazione Volontari Ospedalieri ☎ 055 425 0126/234 4567
- Pharmacies are indicated by a large green or red cross.
- All-night pharmacies: Comunale 13 della Stazione ✉ At the train station ☎ 055 216 761; All'insegna del Moro-Taverna ✉ Piazza San Giovanni 20r ☎ 055 211 343; Molteni ✉ Via dei Calzaivoli 7r ☎ 055 215 472; Paglicci ✉ Via della Scala 61 ☎ 055 215 612. Rota system ☎ 167 420 707 (freephone) for details.

Precautions

- Take care of wallets and handbags as pickpockets target tourists.
- Keep the receipts and numbers of your traveller's cheques separately from the traveller's cheques.
- Keep a copy of the front page of your passport.
- List the numbers and expiry dates of your credit cards and keep the list separately.
- If a theft occurs, make a statement (*denuncia*) at a police station within 24 hours if you wish to make an insurance claim.

LANGUAGE

- Italian pronunciation is totally consistent. *C*s and *g*s are hard when they are followed by an *a*, *o* or *u* (as in 'cat' and 'got'), and soft if followed by an *e* or an *i* (as in 'child' or 'geranium').
- The Tuscans often pronounce their *c*s and *ch*s as *h*s.

Useful words and phrases

good morning	buon giorno
good afternoon/ evening	buona sera
good night	buona notte
hello/goodbye (informal)	ciao
goodbye (informal)	arrivederci
goodbye (formal)	arrivederla
please	per favore
thank you	grazie
you're welcome	prego
how are you?	come sta/stai?
I'm fine	sto bene
I'm sorry	mi dispiace
excuse me/ I beg your pardon	scusi/scusa
excuse me (in a crowd)	permesso

Basic vocabulary

yes	sì
no	no
I do not understand	non ho capito
left	sinistra
right	destra
entrance	entrata
exit	uscita
open	aperto
closed	chiuso
good	buono
bad	cattivo
big	grande
small	piccolo
with	con
without	senza
more	più
less	meno

near	vicino
far	lontano
hot	caldo
cold	freddo
here	qui/qua
there	là/li
today	oggi
tomorrow	domani
yesterday	ieri
how much is it?	quant'è?
when?	quando?
do you have...?	avete...?

Emergencies

help!	aiuto!
where is the nearest telephone?	dov'è il telefono più vicino?
there has been an accident	c'è stato un incidente
call the police	chiamate la polizia
call a doctor/an ambulance	chiamate un medico/ un'ambulanza
first aid	pronto soccorso
where is the nearest hospital?	dov'è l'ospedale più vicino?

Numbers

1/first	uno/primo
2/second	due/secondo
3/third	tre/terzo
4/fourth	quattro/quarto
5/fifth	cinque/quinto
6	sei
7	sette
8	otto
9	nove
10	dieci
20	venti
50	cinquanta
100	cento
1,000	mille
1,000,000	milione

Index

CityPack
Florence

ABOUT THE AUTHOR

Susannah Perry first fell in love with Florence when she was living in Italy as a teenager. She later spent six years taking tourists around the city as well as introducing them to the other major sights of Italy. Susannah now lives in London, where she is a qualified guide. She also writes and lectures on Chinese ceramics, as well as teaching the history of London to American undergraduates. These days she visits Florence purely for pleasure.

CONTRIBUTIONS TO LIVING FLORENCE Sally Roy
THIRD EDITION UPDATED BY Tim Jepson
COVER DESIGN Tigist Getachew, Fabrizio La Rocca
MAPS © Automobile Association Developments Limited 1997, 1999, 2002
FOLD-OUT MAP © Mairs Geographischer Verlag, Germany 2002

A CIP catalogue record for this book is available from the British Library.

ISBN 0 7495 3224 6

Published by AA Publishing (a trading name of Automobile Association Developments Limited, whose registered office is Millstream, Maidenhead Road, Windsor, Berkshire, SL4 5GD. Registered number 1878835).

© **AUTOMOBILE ASSOCIATION DEVELOPMENTS LIMITED 1997, 1999, 2002**
First published 1997. Revised second edition 1999
Revised third edition 2002

Colour separation by Daylight Colour Art Pte Ltd, Singapore
Printed and bound by Dai Nippon Printing Co (Hong Kong) Ltd.

ACKNOWLEDGEMENTS
The Automobile Association would like to thank the following photographers, libraries and associations for their assistance in the preparation of this book. AKG LONDON 16/7; BASILICA DI SANTA CROCE 48b; THE BRIDGEMAN ART LIBRARY, LONDON 16l Palazzo Vecchio (Palazzo della Signoria) Florence, Italy, 16r Museo de Firenze Com'era, Florence, Italy, 16b British Museum, London, UK, 26t Brancacci Chapel, Santa Maria del Carmine, Florence, 26b Brancacci Chapel, Santa Maria del Carmine, Florence, 28b Palazzo Pitti, Florence, 40, Galleria degli Uffizi, Florence, 46a & 46b Museo di San Marco dell'Angelico, Florence; MARY EVANS PICTURE LIBRARY 41b; GETTYONE/STONE 61; ROBERT HARDING PICTURE LIBRARY 7r, 10/1, 15r, 18l; HULTON GETTY 17r; INSTITUTO E MUSEO DI STORIA DELLA SCIENZA 41t; MUSEO DELL'OPERA DEL DUOMO 38b; SPECTRUM COLOUR LIBRARY 48t; STOCKBYTE 5. All remaining pictures are held in the Association's own library (AA PHOTO LIBRARY) and were taken by CLIVE SAWYER with the exception of the following: JERRY EDMANSON cover: guard on scooter, 6r, 32b, 37b, 38t, 39b, 43t, 44t, 45t, 49b, 53t, 55t; SIMON MCBRIDE 1b, 8bl, 8bc, 8br, 8/9, 9r, 9bl, 9br, 10tr, 10l, 11t, 11b, 12tr, 12l, 12/3, 13tl, 13tr, 13r, 1tr, 14l, 14r, 15tr, 15l, 8tr, 18r, 19tl, 19tr, 19r, 19cr, 22tc, 22tl, 22tr, 51t, 51b, 63t, 63b; KEN PATERSON 8l, 15tl, 19l, 20/1, 21t, 36b, 56, 57, 59, 60; BARRIE SMITH 7l; TONY SOUTER 62.

TITLES IN THE CITYPACK SERIES
- Amsterdam • Bangkok • Barcelona • Beijing • Berlin • Boston • Brussels & Bruges •
- Chicago • Dublin • Florence • Hong Kong • Lisbon • Ljubljana • London • Los Angeles •
- Madrid • Melbourne • Miami • Montréal • Munich • New York • Paris • Prague • Rome •
- San Francisco • Seattle • Shanghai • Singapore • Sydney • Tokyo • Toronto • Venice •
- Vienna • Washington •